Escape Velocity

Fighting the Gravitational Pull of Failure

M. Max Boroumand
&
Charlene Boroumand

A 2020 boroumand - A Mediart Company edition

Published in the United States by
boroumand - A Mediart Company
www.boroumand.com

Cover Design: M. Max Boroumand

Based on U.S. Patent No. 10,748,100

ISBN-13 (Paperback): 978-0-9969496-7-5
ISBN-13 (Hardback): 978-0-9969496-8-2

Contents

To our Boys with Love:

When you call yourselves an expert,

you've stopped learning.

Prebabble

Having gone through the scenario depicted in *figure #1* hundreds of times, if not every time, we felt compelled to share our account of how you can avoid the confines of deception and failure, and to write a book that was honest and not self-absorbed.

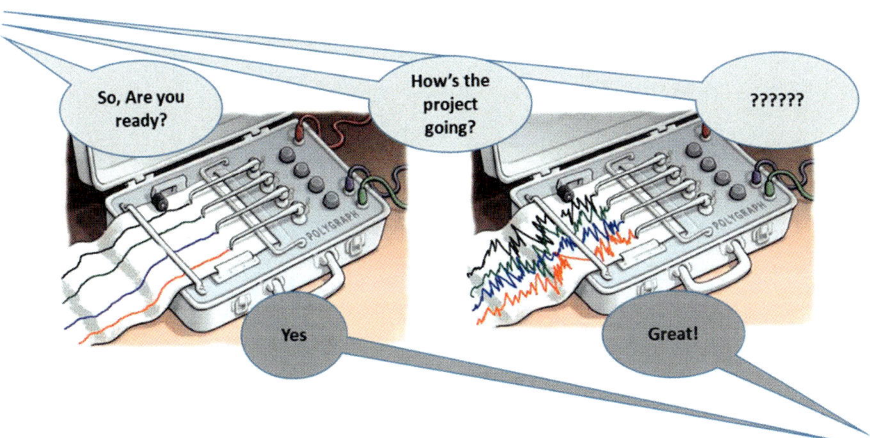

Figure 1 - Lies

Before we go deep into our solution, let's examine the book landscape by looking at books on *investments* as an example.

Books on *personal investments and money management* now number over 10,000 on Amazon, with thousands more published yearly. Many have read more of these than they should.

For those who have read none, let us summarize a majority of them:

Save early and often.

Save more than you spend.

Invest and diversify.

Buy low and sell high.

BOOM... you're done.

Few add anything new to the collective intelligence. There are exceptional books on technical and fundamental analysis, the math, and science behind investing, and other procedural books, which we enjoy, and that have a place on your bookshelf.

In addition, there are some great anecdotal fun reads. However, they're of little value for helping you get ready for retirement. Nevertheless, they allow you to fantasize and live vicariously through those who made it big.

It makes you think, though. *Can there be 10,000+ ways of accomplishing investment and money management? Could there be that many insights beyond all previous offerings?*

Even if there were insights that are new, we would venture to say that one or two pages out of every hundred are worth reading. They should write the books where one page references previous works and the other nine pages are the fresh material. They should be pamphlets[1]!

[1] Any critical reviews about this book probably came from the 10,000+ money management book authors. Just saying!

So, what do the previous bits have to do with this book?

First, we wanted to save you money by having you avoid said books, and more importantly, to point out our philosophy with *this* book.

- It *will* be as short as possible and we will not *bloviate*.
- It *will* be a *fresh* way of thinking and a *fun* read.
- We *will not* judge your methodologies of choice or the tools you use. Nor will we compare and contrast the myriad of both that exist out there. We are tools and methods agnostic.
- Finally, this is our attempt at writing an honest book about *failure,* focusing on *risks* and *returns*, and *investments* companies make in their *people*, *process*, and *assets*, the latter including technologies. This book is about avoiding failure, not about the consequences of failure. We want this book to add to your collective knowledge, with value far beyond its purchase price.

■ ■ ■

Our book was born out of decades of hands-on experience at top consulting firms including Price Waterhouse, Ernst & Young, Computer Sciences Corp (CSC), and CSC-Index, at various start-ups, and the Fortune 500, working on significant projects with splendid people.

The above experiences became the foundation for our patented process and software, "**Method and Apparatus for Enterprise Investment Delivery and Value Assurance**[2]" and the basis for this book.

We enhanced the process with surveys of thousands of executives and managers, hundreds of interviews, and many dozens of audits of companies on the ways *they* managed *projects*, *programs*, and *portfolios*.

[2] First Issue 2014; Second Issue August 2020 (U.S. Patent No. 10,748,100)

■ ■ ■

We performed our audits, interviews, and surveys as part of our management consulting and SAAS offerings, encompassing the following service categories:

- Portfolio Management
- Program and Portfolio Management Audits
- Asset Class & Asset Type Evaluation and Standardization
- Portfolio and Program Management Effectiveness
- Risk Assessments & Failure Analysis
- Management and Manager Assessments
- Data Analytics and Business Analysis

We covered various industries including Health Care, Consumer Goods, Financial and Banking, Software, Utilities, Energy, etc., in geographies including U.S.A., Canada, Europe, Australia, and the Middle East, encompassing business units such as Finance, Information Technology (IT), Marketing, Manufacturing, etc., with portfolio & program sizes ranging from $1 million to over $50 million, and several multi-billion dollar outsourcing projects.

We conducted our structured and unstructured surveys anonymously; before, during, and/or after engagements, with both open-ended and closed-ended questions, putting significant effort into making the surveys balanced and statistically significant.

The data collected over the decades refined our processes, with special emphasis on our assurance process and the inner workings of our portfolio management capabilities.

■ ■ ■

We shall present more of the data collected in our "Bonus II" chapter covering surveys, Machine Learning (ML) and data analytics, further reinforcing our conclusions.

■ ■ ■

Lastly, we wrote this book in a style different from most business books to make it a pleasurable read. We hope you enjoy it and learn something new and valuable. Please contact[3] us to share your thoughts, ideas, and to ask questions.

---

[3] The best way to get in touch with us is through our LinkedIn profiles. Connect and write us a note.

Babble

What is Escape Velocity and what do we mean by fighting the gravitational pull of failure?

> Fail.ure (/ˈfālyər/) - Lack of Success. The action or state of not functioning. The sudden cessation of power. The collapse of a business.

Failure is the natural state of things with its own innate gravitational pull. All things creep towards failure. Think of your health, house, car, and most other items you purchase, from clothing to food. They all move towards a state of failure, a state of uselessness, ineffectiveness, or cessation of power.

> Es.cape Ve.loc.i.ty (/əˈskāp vəˌläsədē/) - the lowest velocity which a body must have in order to escape the gravitational attraction of a particular planet, other objects [or events.]

Escape velocity, in our treatment, would be the minimum[4] you have to do to break from the inherent gravitational pull as relates to an object or event whose value you wish to maximize.

[4] e.g., refrigerating your food, maintaining your car, caring for your health by eating well and exercising, painting your house, etc.

This book is about applying the concepts of escape velocity to the projects you undertake and introducing a framework for fighting the gravitational pull of failure in your projects.

Project Management has a lengthy history going back to the Incan and Egyptian pyramids, Persepolis, the Great Wall of China, and even earlier. Project management applies knowledge, skills, tools, and techniques to a class of activities to meet stated objectives and requirements.

To enhance performance, people develop *new* methodologies, tools, and techniques yearly, and spend significantly on software to help automate it all. On top of that, they've created broad *Program* and *Portfolio Management* capabilities, where *programs* are a grouping of projects or investments, and *portfolios* are a grouping of programs, theoretically.

Companies embark on so many projects every year that during the early 2000s, a new industry erupted to help manage them called *Project Portfolio Management* (PPM). Most if not all large companies implemented some variation of the capability offered by one of a dozen small software companies. In time, big software companies consumed these small software companies, and now PPM is part of *their* Enterprise Resource Planning (ERP) suite of software and services.

So now there are dozens of methodologies and many desktop or SAAS solutions supporting project, program, and portfolio management. In addition, there are many certification programs including PMP, CPM, PgMP, PfMP, CAPM, ACP, CSM, PRINCE2, etc., comprising various approaches and aspects of managing projects.

Project management is a *critical* necessity for any organization. We shall not debate this. Nor will we debate the need for program or portfolio management.

Yet, projects keep failing.

▪ ▪ ▪

We have been studying projects for a decade before and a decade after the height of the Portfolio Management business fad. Sadly, it has had little to no effect on the landscape. The statistics before and after implementing Program and Portfolio Management have barely changed. In the case of projects:

- 80± % fail in at least one of:
    - On Time Delivery;
    - Budget;
    - Meeting Capabilities or Objectives.
- 90± % are not sufficiently aware of each other, resulting in conflict, minimal collaboration, and wasted resources.
- 68± % cannot link directly or measurably to business objectives or targets.

The core capabilities of true portfolio management are not present in any of the audited or surveyed companies. It appears implementing PPM capabilities simply automated existing destructive behaviors, including:

- Self-reported, bottom-up subjective statuses
- Reactive and repair-oriented responses
- Creating Initiatives as cost accounts
- Building GIGO[5] information models

[5] Garbage In, Garbage Out.

As it turns out, PPM tools are nothing more than *inventory management* systems; a centralized system for collecting and reporting on projects and allocating resources. We never saw signs of *true portfolio management*, using any of the modern portfolio theories or any cogent analytics for evaluating, selecting, or retiring investments. That is to say, there were plenty of ways to disavow a project on obvious grounds, but nothing logical or formulaic for evaluating a series of well-crafted investments in the running.

In several cases, we found managers who had developed bitwise selection or voting processes, similar to choosing pizza toppings amongst friends at a super bowl party.

> *"OK, so that'll be 3 with pepperoni and olives, 5 with pepperoni, onions, and green pepper, 2 with ham and pineapple, 4 with ground beef and mushrooms, 6 meat combos, 4 veggie combos, and 1 plain cheese.... F*ck it, we'll just get 20 combos and you guys can pick the sh*t off you don't like. That's how we do it."*
>
> Survey Respondent #202

These companies developed voting systems that never worked as intended but only regulated internal control and power issues by allowing people to opine and baselessly prioritize, with nothing connected to objectives. Their mistaken assumptions were that the people voting had, within their own priorities, an understanding of objectives, goals, and corporate needs.

In one survey, we asked, "*At your level, do you trust the decisions of the people one, two, and three levels above you?*" The further away, the less they trusted or believed that decisions were being made soundly. Over 63% did not trust the decisions at all three levels above them.

"In this company, there is an erroneous assumption that decisions inherently include analytics and logic, and are rational." Survey Respondent #6173

When asked, *"Looking down one, two, or three levels, do you think they trust and believe in your decisions?"* The responses were *yes* all the way down. Twenty-four percent (24%) believed people beneath them trusted them fully at all levels. The majority (73%) trusted them regularly at all levels.

"I don't believe or trust anyone above me. I think everyone below me believes and trusts me…" Survey Respondent #3915

It's no wonder projects fail. There is little trust in one direction and assumed trust in the other. Up and down many corporate trees, the feelings were unvaryingly equal to the above-mentioned sentiments.

WHY THE CONTINUED FAILURE?

There are many reasons projects/investments fail. We won't spend time on the most obvious reasons, such as lack of proper funding, poor resourcing, skills deficits, internal strife and conflict, or any of a dozen common ways investments fail from poor planning.

We want to focus on investments whose failures are a surprise to the leadership. The ones that sneak up on you during or after the fact, emphasizing failure points.

So why *do* projects fail?

*"... the reason our projects fail is because we don't give a sh*t about them."* Survey Respondent #8

"WTF?" you blurt bewildered and upset you paid for this book.

■ ■ ■

We heard this repeatedly at so many companies. We think this response holds true at many levels requiring deep examination. You can gloss over this all you want, call it cynical, or over the top. It's the truth as some people see it when, for many years, they've worked hard, suffered late nights, missed special life events, but no longer understand what drove them to make those sacrifices and don't believe it was worth it.

We have spent years working on many dozens of *consultancy* projects across a diverse set of industries and have loved most of them. They have been a great source of personal growth, they were consequential, they were unique, and they included great people with whom we became friends.

"Did the projects succeed? Did any project ever come in on budget or on time? Did you meet the objectives?" You ask.

- From our perspective, as consultants, we succeeded, learned, and grew.
- From the consultancies' perspective, they made money, lots of money, trained their staff, and gained a reference.
- From the client's or venture capital's perspective, consultants met objectives but *scarcely* came in on time or on budget, (when not using our framework.)

- From the client employee's perspective, the spectrum was broad. At one end, some hated the consultants and everything they stood for, and on the other end, it was a great learning experience and they loved it. *But did they think it was a success?* That too covers wide-ranging answers, but mostly yes.

Success is a matter of perspective.

Here is a blurb from one interview, not unique, and part of a comprehensive interview we conducted with project managers.

"*... You are being paid a salary to be a project manager,*" we said to a client project manager.

"*Yes, I'm paid to manage projects, not guarantee success,*" the manager replied.

"*What's the difference? Isn't that your job?*"

"*To be successful, I have to manage my part, AND be involved in making sure all the other connected parts are successful, and that everyone else is also successful... I'm not paid enough to do everyone's job.*"

"*Would you do your job perfectly, if everyone else did their job perfectly?*"

"*Yes, but that'll never happen. Plus, we really don't have a real interest in doing anything beyond our own job. We do the absolute minimum plus a little more to make sure we keep our job and get our raises... That's life.*"

This fragment of dialog was repeated in many forms, at differing experience levels, and differing tenures. Sometimes it was anger and frustration. However, most times people who liked their jobs, co-workers, bosses, and work life balance offered it notwithstanding. They merely stated the above as fact.

It is what it is. Or is it?

It is a lack of engagement, but more importantly, we believe there is a fundamental difference in the belief systems between people who have a personal stake in the outcome of a project and those who do not. Outcomes can be personal and go beyond pay. It could include learning something of value, being part of something great, or believing the work will ultimately be far-reaching and consequential.

Emotional connection to your work is critical and changes behaviors.

We behave differently when we manage a *work-related* project versus when we manage our own *personal* projects. The difference is fundamentally about our point of view on ***risks*** and ***returns***. It boils down to a simple paradigm difference based on which end of the failure spectrum you begin your project.

With personal projects, we understand failure's inherent gravitational pull and mitigate accordingly, most of the time.

WHAT IS FAILURE?

For *projects*, failure is not meeting *some* or *all* of your *objectives* with failure correlating to the number of objectives not met. Most *corporate* projects (Figure 2) begin with an implicit assumption of success and then slog their way towards partial or total *failure*.

Figure 2 - Corporate Paradigm

They propose a project, set the timeline, establish resource needs, set the price, and add schedule and cost buffers. They run a kick-off meeting, filled with joy, confidence, and anticipation of their eventual success. It rarely, if ever, ends the way they imagined, planned, or proposed.

▪ ▪ ▪

Yet, we do the exact opposite for *personal* situations (Figure 3) such as buying a used car or a home, or similar expensive endeavors. We turn the process around 180 degrees.

Figure 3 - Personal Paradigm

We begin with the assumption that the purchase is implicitly faulty, will fail, and has something (or many things) wrong with it. We then proceed from that initial perspective of partial or total *failure* to purposefully and methodically work our way towards *success*.

Let's explore buying a *used car* to illustrate the point.

▪ ▪ ▪

When we buy a *used car*, we assume the car is not as advertised, a good assumption since they rarely are. Therefore, we go into the deal cautiously and take intentional actions we believe will mitigate our risk. We *inspect* the car, we *test drive* it and, if it passes, we move to the next set of steps. We check its *history* and take it to a *mechanic*. Finally, when the risk mitigation steps are complete, we negotiate and perhaps make a deal. In short, we assume the used car is a piece of junk, a failure, and then we diligently work to disprove that assumption by mitigating risk, proving the opposite, and moving us towards a successfully negotiated purchase.

We start our journey on the side of *failure*. Not only that, we continuously and progressively keep mitigating risk, by doing scheduled maintenance, rotating and buying new tires, keeping up with insurance and registration payments, etc. As the car ages, it reintroduces risk, moving our investment back towards the failure end of the spectrum. We must continuously monitor and take action to move it towards success where it is risk-mitigated and achieves positive returns over its useful lifetime.

Failure has a gravitational pull that success does not.

We're not saying that corporate, business, and work-related projects do not mitigate and manage risk, or that they do not take into account failures and failure points. We say that they start at the wrong end of the *failure spectrum*. They start with the assumption of success and then react to the indicators that show evidence for it moving towards partial or total failure.

Back to the used car. If you think of a used car and its working *components*, they all have a time value variable we'll call a *half-life*[6]. The used car, or any investment, naturally moves towards failure as its underlying *components* reach their *half-life*, similar to a freshness expiry date on food, and the risk of failure marginally increases by a specific amount. It is failure's gravitational pull that must be proactively and continuously managed.

■ ■ ■

This correct behavior, starting investment efforts under the unflattering and difficult assumption that failure is intrinsically present, is readily manifested in start-ups and incubation businesses. In start-ups where employees had stock options, a financial interest, or were on the cusp of something unique and new, they behaved more in line with personal projects. Having a stake in the game and a meaningful outcome tied to you and a team of people you care about personally, are all drivers of better results.

When there is a direct positive correlation between the outcomes and one's own personal standing, the *failure spectrum rotates*, and we willingly fight against failure's natural gravitational pull. Because we *want* to win.

In business, projects are

a success until they're not.

In real life, it's the opposite.

Unfortunately, in most cases, companies struggle to offer employees any more than their salaries, the projects may not be inherently interesting, or there's little new to learn, yet people must do their jobs.

---

[6] Technically, half-life is the time required for a quantity to reduce to half of its initial value. In this context it represents the time any existing component is contributing to a marginal reduction in the chance of failure. Once elapsed, risk goes up again.

HOW DO YOU PREVENT FAILURES?

The solution is simple, but not easy. If you cannot change the way people do the work, change the way *you* review the work. Reverse the way you look at and manage your investments. Start from the failure side of the spectrum. Treat every project as though you're buying a used car and will drive it yourself and get the team to think similarly.

Reverse the paradigm, change your framework.

We have become good at costing projects and identifying what needs to be done. We have to become great at costing projects when what needs to be done does not get done or is undone.

Buying a Used Car

Let's build this *framework* from the ground up by first focusing on the questions you ask and answer in most every investment. We shall explore the *used car* venture as almost everyone can relate to or knows someone who can relate to this common endeavor.

ADDING DIMENSIONS

Every investment that you make has an ***event horizon*** (Figure 4) (i.e., a "point of no return" or perhaps a go-live date when cash inflows or other returns and benefits accrue,) with specific categories or ***dimensions*** of activities occurring both before the event horizon (i.e., *strategic* and *tactical*,) and after it (i.e., *operational*.) The event horizon is the logical demarcation line.

In buying a used car, the *event horizon* is the moment you exchange your money for their title and car.

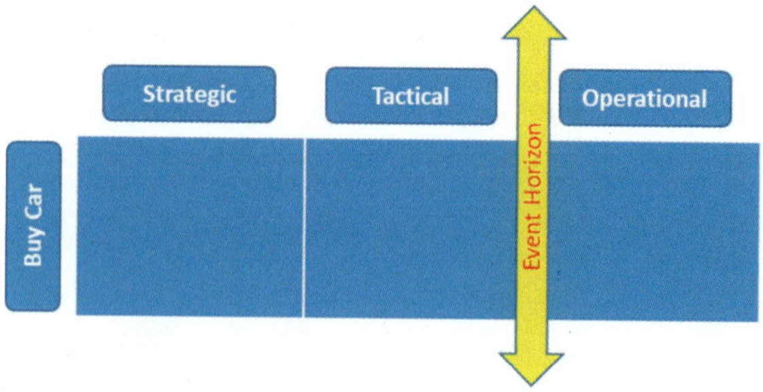

Figure 4 - Simple Framework

The framework's dimensions include…

Strategic – All the steps and processes that help you move forward with an investment or project, e.g.

- Should I buy a used car?
- Can I afford it?
- Do I need it?

Tactical – All the steps and processes that help you build, select, refine, change, and add to the investment or project, e.g.

- What model of used car should I try to buy?
- Where do I look for the car?
- Driving, inspecting, and evaluating the car…

Event Horizon – The point of no return e.g., buying the car.

Operational – All the steps and processes that help you maintain and extract maximum value from the investment or project, and that keep it from failing, e.g.

- Registering and insuring the car,
- Driving the car,
- Maintaining the car; including oil changes, tire rotations, etc.

The framework is circular and bidirectional. At any point and in any dimension, the investment can discontinue. It could also continue by moving back into the earlier phase and starting anew, or by spawning new branches that represent a unique aspect in the lifespan of the original investment (e.g., divestment.)

ADDING COMPONENTS AND PROCESS

The next step in developing the *framework* is to break down investment analysis and management by identifying ***components*** that fit into each of the dimensions: Strategic, Tactical, and Operational. *Components* are the minimum required success elements for the investment, which answer your questions, and give you confidence, or ***assurance,*** in the ultimate success of the investment.

Components not only help in shaping the investment by answering your questions but also help identify potential *points of failure.* They may be as simple as checking off items from a list, to a formal review by a professional, to a physical act like driving the car. Each *component* should help answer specific questions as prescribed by the dimension.

Collectively they should answer *all* the questions, across *all* the dimensions, throughout the life cycle, from cradle to grave.

Since you may do this again for your next used car or for a friend or for your children, codify this effort into an ***Asset Type*** called "Buying a Used Car." By doing so, you and others, can reuse this framework every time one is considering buying a used car.

Strategic Component	Exists
Car Needs Assessment and Objectives List	Y
Financial Assessment (TCO)	Y
Financing (Optional)	N/A

Tactical Component	Exists
Inventory Check and Sorting	Y
Short Listing, Scheduling and Logistics	Y
Initial Personal Physical Inspection Checklist	Y
Final Professional Inspection Checklist (Optional)	N
Negotiations Steps and Checklist	Y
Final Transaction Checklist	Y

Operational Component	Exists
Register and Insure Car	Y
Maintain Car	Y
Re-assess Risk/Returns	N

Figure 5 - Components

Notably, we call analyzing and evaluating the components ***Delivery & Value Assurance***, where:

- **Delivery Assurance** | Getting a project or investment to the Event Horizon, and ongoing assertions of continued achievement of the stated requirements and objectives post-Event Horizon.
- **Value Assurance** | Maximizing the value of a project and investment before and after the Event Horizon by minimizing costs and maximizing returns.

Delivery and Value Assurance is a systematic set of processes or steps that enable stakeholders to iteratively and progressively reduce ***Risk*** and reduce variances in ***Returns*** (i.e., costs and benefits) over the life of the investment.

ABOUT RISK

Risk has two variables:

Uncertainty and Exposure

Uncertainty is the probability of failure, or a failure event, for a given type of investment adjusted for the current state of one's capabilities to deliver on the components of the investment. If you are an experienced car mechanic across a broad range of car models, your level of capability to deliver on the components of the Asset Type called *Buying a Used Car* is likely higher than ours and so our probability of the used car investment failing to achieve our cost & benefit requirements and our overall objectives, our *uncertainty,* is likely higher than yours.

Exposure is a liability multiple that would arise from an occurrence of failure. It represents the magnitude of the impact resulting from a failure, typically a multiple of originally expected costs.

If either or both variables are not present,

there is no risk.

For example, if a man jumps out of an airplane with a parachute on his back, he may be uncertain whether the chute will open. His *risk* is high because he is highly *exposed* to that *uncertainty*. If the chute cannot open, he will suffer personally.

In the same example, spectators on the ground may be equally *uncertain* whether the chute will open, but they have no personal *exposure* to that uncertainty (hopefully), therefore there is no *risk*.

In the same example once more, if the man is jumping from ten feet up, the *uncertainty* of the chute not opening remains the same, or the chute may not even open, but the *exposure* is low, therefore, there is no *risk*. Therefore,

$$Risk = Probability_{Event} * Cost_{Event}$$

or

$$Risk = P(E) * C(E)$$

Keep *risk* low by eliminating or reducing at least one of the two variables, preferably both. Either reduce or eliminate probability of an event occurring (*uncertainty*) or reduce or eliminate the cost associated with the event occurrence (*exposure*).

Keep in mind, each *component* has a *half-life*. Know the time each component will maintain its value to the investment and its expiration date and know the incremental or marginal *Risk* that is reintroduced by the expiration of that component.

The lack of attention to component's half-life is the principal reason many projects fail while in the operational phase, post *event-horizon*. After all, who's interested in amending the data model, updating the testing scripts, or adjusting the process maps? When an event occurs, and they always do, demanding work on an investment few of the *components* are up-to-date and of value.

For each component (Figure 6, Figure 7) have at a minimum, P(E) and C(E) measures with subjective Low, Medium, or High values, or with a range [1..5] or [1..10].

Time Value

Existence

Strategic Component	Half-Life	Exists	P(E)	C(E)
Car Needs Assessment and Objectives List	12 mos.	Y	L	L
Financial Assessment (TCO)	6 mos.	Y	L	L
Financing (Optional)	N/A	N/A	L	L

Probability of Event introducing failure points

The cost/exposure to said failure points

Figure 6 - Component Detail

However, for best results, use percentages, where P(E) is a value greater than 0% and less than 100%, and C(E) is a value greater than zero (0%.) For example,

- P(E) = 50% implies there is a 50% chance that failure points, as defined by the components and representing the chance of the event happening over the life of the investment, will be introduced into the risk profile.
- C(E) = 210% implies that failure points may increase the investment cost by as much as 210% of initial estimates.
- Expired or non-existent components mean their marginal risk is included (or re-included) in the overall investment risk profile.

Strategic Component	Half-Life	Exists	P(E)	C(E)
Car Needs Assessment and Objectives List	12 mos.	Y	L	L
Financial Assessment (TCO)	6 mos.	Y	L	L
Financing (Optional)	N/A	N/A	L	L

Tactical Component	Half-Life	Exists	P(E)	C(E)
Inventory Check and Sorting	12 mos.	Y	L	L
Short Listing, Scheduling and Logistics	6 mos..	Y	L	L
Initial Personal Physical Inspection Checklist	1 day	Y	M	M
Final Professional Inspection Checklist (Optional)	6 mos.	N	H	H
Negotiations Steps and Checklist	1 day	Y	L	L
Final Transaction Checklist	1 day	Y	L	L

Operational Component	Half-Life	Exists	P(E)	C(E)
Register and Insure Car	12 mos.	Y	L	H
Maintain Car	12 mons.	Y	M	M
Re-assess Risk/Returns	6 mos.	N	L	M

Figure 7 - Components by Dimension

In the used car scenario, your initial physical inspection of the car may be valid only for the next six or twelve months, longer if the car is newer and less if the car is sufficiently old, after which the true state of the used car may become suspect once again.

Your monthly insurance payment is only of value for that month, after which you are putting yourself at severe *risk* with a major downside potential to your *returns*. A $3000 used car may cost you $100,000 in liabilities, or worse, should you have an accident with injuries or death.

ABOUT RETURNS

We use *Returns* in the broadest sense. It must be a quantifiable measure that eventually has a positive effect or value.

$$Cash_{In} - Cash_{Out} > Zero$$

Some investments may, for a long time, only have negative values (i.e., cash outflows only,) but attempt to minimize them or, better yet, attach them to one or more corporate objectives that are quantifiable in the positive (e.g., a 20% contribution [yours] to a 5% reduction [total] in Cost of Goods Sold.)

Overall, every investment should return value, either in the form of a positive cash flow, reduction of costs, or a positive effect on one or more corporate objectives.

Tie all investments directly to objectives.

Back to the used car investment.

The assurance process does not allow time for reviewing the details of each component. Nor are we responsible for creating components. We check their *existence*. At the start of any *assurance process*, there must be a template, sample, or creation method for each *component*, against which we evaluate its *existence*.

A component *exists*, if and only if it is...

- *Complete* in its content relative to the blueprint or template;
- *Accessible* and known to everyone who needs it; **and**
- *Up-to-date* and valid for current conditions.

If a *component* does not *exist*, the incremental risk associated with its non-existence is introduced (i.e., added) back into total investment risk. Again, as mentioned before, *expiration* of a component nullifies its existence, introducing the incremental risk back in *automatically*. Existence does not necessarily eliminate *risk*. It stands to minimize *risk* or point out other points of failure or additional *risks*.

The assurance process follows these steps for each component:

1. *Is it accessible on demand?* If you have to go digging and asking around for it for some time, then it does not exist.
2. *Do those who need it have it?* Tell me who needs to have access to this content, and if we call them and they say they don't know where it is, then it does not exist.
3. *Is it up-to-date, complete, and fits the prescribed blueprint?* This step is the more time-consuming part of the assurance process. It is the step whereby you compare the output against the sample or blueprint and allocate parts of the incremental risk back into the total risk profile for the investment based on degrees of disparity. This step requires subject matter expertise, a SME.

■ ■ ■

To the used car buying investment again. We've taken the "Initial Personal Inspection Checklist" (Figure 8) component and expanded it into a complete list, an evaluation checklist. If sufficient items in the evaluation checklist are not checked off, you add the full *component* incremental risk back into the total investment risk, which for a car could be high. In essence, you are buying the car sight unseen. If the list is evaluated fully, you may take that incremental risk value and reduce it with each successful check mark on the list.

Therefore, in defining components in your framework, consider these factors and give the risk variable appropriate values beyond just low (L, or Green), medium (M, or Yellow), or high (H, or Red.)

We recommend using percentages for greater accuracy.

Exterior	Yes	No
Windshield free of cracks		
Body panel colors match		
Magnet adheres to all steel body panels		
Fresh paint job (if yes, it could be to conceal rust)		
Seams where the trunk and hood close are properly aligned		
Seams where doors and fenders meet are properly aligned		
Free of body scratches		
Free of body dents		
Windshields wipers and blades fully functional		
Headlights and directional lights intact and fully functional		
Tires		
Tires are a reputable brand name (Michelin, Bridgestone, Goodyear)		
Tires are all of the same make		
Tires are of free of any cuts, bubbles or cracks		
Tread worn evenly		
Spare tire, jack and lug wrench on car and fully functional		
Spare tire inflated		
Engine		
Free of fluid or oil leaks		
Oil filler neck not coated with thick, black deposits		
Battery terminals free of corrosion		
Oil dip stick free of dark, black oil		
Free of odors while engine is running		
Exhaust pipe emissions are neither blue or black		
Suspensions		
Vehicle rests levelly		
When bouncing the vehicle's corners, no creaking noises are made		
All corners respond the same when bouncing		
Frame		
Chassis is neither bent nor cracked		
No signs of crumpling or straightening inside the trunk		
Frame holes just inside outer edge clean and free of scratches		
Automatic Transmission		
Transmission fluid looks clean, not dirty or gritty		
Transmission neither slips nor delays when driving		
Manaul Transmission		
Each gear shifts smoothly		
No grinding noises when in reverse		
Brakes		
Vehicle steers straight and does not pull to one side when applying brakes		
Parking brake engages and disengages freely		
No grinding noises when applying		
Wheels do not lock when applying antilock brakes (if applicable)		
Steering		
Vehicle does not drift to one side without prodding		
Vehicle is stable; no shaking or vibrating		
No resistance in the steering wheel when turning		
No clicking or clunking when turning		

Interiror	Yes	No
Seats unworn and free of cracks		
All doors open and close freely		
Trunk opens and closes freely		
Lacks a heavy scent of air freshener		
All gauges work		
No dashboard warning lights remain illuminated		
Stereo works		
Heater works		
Air conditioner works		
Windshield wipers work		
Windshield wiper fluid dispenses properly		
All seats equipped with functional seat belts		
All seats adjust properly		
Power windows operate properly		
Sunroof opens and closes properly (if applicable)		
Car alarm works (if applicable)		
Trunk and driver-side door lock and unlock with key		
Hazard lights function properly		
Headlights, including brights, work properly		
Frame		
Chassis is neither bent nor cracked		
No signs of crumpling or straightening inside the trunk		
Frame holes just inside outer edge clean and free of scratches		
Automatic Transmission		
Transmission fluid looks clean, not dirty or gritty		
Transmission neither slips nor delays when driving		
Manaul Transmission		
Each gear shifts smoothly		
No grinding noises when in reverse		
Brakes		
Vehicle steers straight and does not pull to one side when applying brakes		
Parking brake engages and disengages freely		
No grinding noises when applying		
Wheels do not lock when applying antilock brakes (if applicable)		
Steering		
Vehicle does not drift to one side without prodding		
Vehicle is stable; no shaking or vibrating		
No resistance in the steering wheel when turning		
No clicking or clunking when turning		
Other		
Car manual located in the glove compartment		
Instructions included for any accessories		
Service and repair records available		
Owner has title		
Other		
Car manual located in the glove compartment		
Instructions included for any accessories		
Service and repair records available		
Owner has title		

Figure 8 - Initial Personal Inspection Checklist

In our used car Asset Type, there are 12 components (Figure 9). If we use ranges, Low-Med-High for P(E) and C(E), in place of broader values as in percentages, we won't be able to gauge risk nearly as accurately.

If we use the LMH scaling, we are giving each component a range between 1 and 9[7] giving us components with risk profiles in proximity to each other. This does not allow for a large enough gap between components and will not allow for proper weighting of risk.

[7] L × L or 1 × 1=1 all the way to H × H or 3 × 3=9

Again, using percentages is best. However, if you have many hundreds of projects and thousands of components, stick to HML.

Strategic Component	Half-Life	Exists	P(E)	C(E)
Car Needs Assessment and Objectives List	12 mos.	Y	1%	1%
Financial Assessment (TCO)	6 mos.	Y	1%	1%
Financing (Optional)	N/A	N/A	1%	1%

Tactical Component	Half-Life	Exists	P(E)	C(E)
Inventory Check and Sorting	12 mos.	Y	1%	1%
Short Listing, Scheduling and Logistics	6 mos..	Y	1%	1%
Initial Personal Physical Inspection Checklist	1 day	Y	50%	100%
Final Professional Inspection Checklist (Optional)	6 mos.	N	50%	300%
Negotiations Steps and Checklist	1 day	Y	1%	1%
Final Transaction Checklist	1 day	Y	1%	1%

Operational Component	Half-Life	Exists	P(E)	C(E)
Register and Insure Car	12 mos.	Y	75%	10,000%
Maintain Car	12 mons.	Y	25%	500%
Re-assess Risk/Returns	6 mos.	N	1%	100%

Figure 9 - Used Car Components

The components "Initial Personal Inspection Checklist" and "Final Professional Physical Inspection Checklist" each have substantially higher risk profiles than the others, therefore overweight those measures to fit a more accurate risk model.

By using percentages, we can focus on those areas that matter most. In the strategic area, there are considerations and questions answered, but none has a consequential risk profile. In the tactical dimension, the two critical components are the initial personal inspection, including the test drive, *and* the mechanic's inspection.

In the operational realm it is the registration, insurance, and maintenance that are critical to the risk model.

COST MULTIPLIER

The Delivery and Value Assurance process results in a *Cost Multiplier* for each component. When applied across all components, it will give you the best estimate of TCO should you NOT mitigate the risks.

Looking at our used car, priced at $3000, focusing on the tactical dimension. We have two items of consequence:

$$Risk_{\substack{Inspect\\Test\ Drive}} = 50\%_{P(E)} * 100\%_{C(E)} * \$3000_{\substack{Car's\\Price}}$$

$$Risk_{\substack{Mechanic's\\Inspection}} = 50\%_{P(E)} * 300\%_{C(E)} * \$3000_{\substack{Car's\\Price}}$$

The consequential tactical risks are $1500 (Test Drive) and $4500 (Mechanic's Inspection).

In the operational dimension, we have two items of consequence:

$$Risk_{\substack{Register\\and\ Insure}} = 75\%_{P(E)} * 10{,}000\%_{C(E)} * \$3000_{\substack{Car's\\Price}}$$

$$Risk_{Maintain\ Car} = 25\%_{P(E)} * 500\%_{C(E)} * \$3000_{\substack{Car's\\Price}}$$

The consequential operational risks are $225,000 (Register and Insure) and $3,750 (Maintain Car).

Several components are purposefully large to illustrate several key points.

- Component risk profiles can be large, forcing junior risk managers to feel as though they have to lower it because it looks out of place. We're here to tell you risk can be proportionally much larger and extreme, as with an uninsured car. Nearly 1.25 million people die in road crashes each year with 20-50 times more people injured.
- Some of the most consequential components with high-risk profiles occur after the Event Horizon, often long after the project team has moved on so keep a lightweight assurance process in place throughout the investment's life cycle.

- Understanding and paying attention to a component's half-life is critical. It allows for automatic re-introduction of risk. Imagine missing an insurance payment and then getting into an accident.
- Having a well-documented set of components with their risk profiles in place are essential before you spend a dime.
- Knowing the risk profile of one component may affect all others. Insurance premiums for a car vary significantly. Thus, that one component may affect a strategic component changing the car model you might seek to purchase.

EVENT HORIZON AND ASSET TYPE SAMPLES

The following lists show you some simple alternative framework usages beyond the used car example which are readily understood by most people.

EVENT HORIZONS

- Opening a Restaurant
- Deploying an ERP system
- Opening New Offices
- A Product Launch
- Buy a House
- Sell a House

CORPORATE ASSET TYPES

- Business Continuity
- Business Process Re-Engineering
- Business Systems Design
- Corporate Security
- COTS Package Deployment
- Credit Risk Management
- Custom Software Development and Deployment
- Divestment
- Large Scale System Services Procurement Machine / Deep Learning
- Mergers and Acquisitions
- Organization Change
- Outsourcing Evaluation
- Performance Engineering and Optimization
- Process Improvement
- Product Launch
- Security Audit
- Staff Planning and Development
- Supply Chain Risk Assessment
- Treasury Risk Management

THE HOTEL EXAMPLE - A QUICK VIEW

Hotels, restaurants, or for that matter any customer facing retail business has a distinct and well know Event Horizon. That is, the day they are open for business.

In our hotel sample, it is the day they are open and can accommodate guests and provide other services.

Pre Event Horizon

- Value Assurance focuses on the viability of this hotel and the ability of it to maintain occupancy and room rates to satisfy the investment returns over the full time horizon.
  - Business Plans, Demand/Supply Analysis, Financing, ROI and IRR Requirements, etc.
- Delivery Assurance focuses on licensing, design, and construction efforts needed to build the hotel within specifications, on time and within budget.
  - Project Plans, Permits and Licensing, Contracting, Build Plans, Electrical Plans, Materials Acquisition, Equipment Leasing, etc.

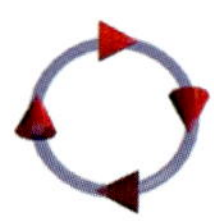

Post Event Horizon

- Value Assurance focuses on the operating costs, revenue streams and related financial performances to assure the value is maintained and adjustments are made.
  - Cash Flow Analysis, Financial Ratio Analysis, etc.
- Delivery Assurance focuses on operations, maintenance, license and certification expiration dates and renewals, and keeping the delivery of all hotel products and services within operational specifications.
  - Staffing, Customer Satisfaction, Repairs, Maintenance, etc.

Delivery and Value Assurance

is a continuous and circular process,

with you entering and exiting

dimensions as you make decisions

focusing on risks and returns

Expand the Framework

How well does your organization assemble new ideas, develop them into initiatives, provide funding for them, identify and mitigate their risks, track and realign their progress and ultimately measure their returns?

Buying a *used car* is a simple investment as compared to a merger or acquisition, building a high rise, or building an enterprise-wide custom software solution catering to a global user and customer base.

When do you decide to terminate an initiative? Do you consider which ideas to invest in based on their expected returns alone or also their potential to uplift returns in other areas?

ADDING DEPTH

To accommodate these complex initiatives and the hundreds of questions asked and answered, we expand the *framework* by adding three more dimensions, *People, Process,* and *Assets,* to our existing ones, *Strategic, Tactical,* and *Operational* (Figure 10).

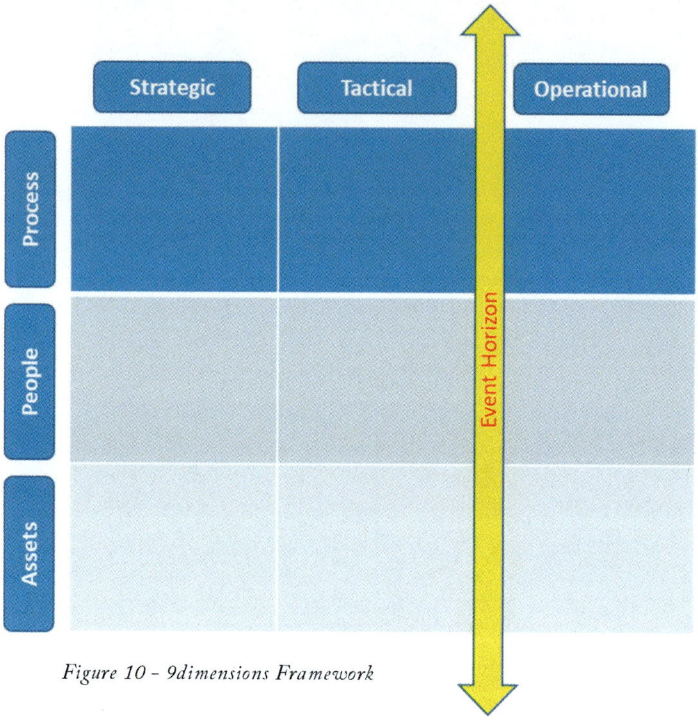

Figure 10 - 9dimensions Framework

With this expansion, we can better place our components, activities and, deliverables, to prepare for the assurance process and *comparative* analysis.

$$Asset\ Type_x^1\ v.Asset\ Type_x^2$$

Similar Asset Types (x), two different projects (1 and 2), or

$$Asset\ Type_x^1\ v.Asset\ Type_y^2$$

Different Asset Types (x and y), two different projects (1 and 2.)

Fundamental to the framework is the principle that you can differentiate and describe investments through understanding and planning its *strategic*, *tactical*, and *operational* influences on *people*, *process*, and *assets*[8].

The investments must align with enterprise or business area objectives *strategically*. It must be developed and implemented *tactically*, and its full benefit achieved *operationally*. This requires careful consideration of each aspect of *process*, *people*, and *asset* components for the Asset Type's (investment's) entire life cycle.

The greatest benefits that result from developing models along the nine dimensional framework (9dimensions®) is that you are much less likely to forget important variables, you can better leverage the categories considered by prior analysts and best of all, you now have a sound and consistent basis for comparing distinct project areas.

Extrapolating these concepts upward to portfolios of investments, we can see how organizing across these 9dimensions sets the baseline for identifying and defining Investment Classes or *Asset Types*.

Assuming you do a good job filling the 9dimensions for any specific investment e.g., Custom Software Development, Mergers and Acquisitions (M&A), etc. you have defined the Asset Type and can use it repeatedly, adjusting for changes as required.

You can compare similar and dissimilar Asset Types across the entire enterprise over time by comparing their 9dimensions framework.

$$\text{Project } A_{\text{Asset Type } x}^{\begin{matrix} Strat\text{-}Proc & Tact\text{-}Proc & Ops\text{-}Proc \\ Strat\text{-}Peo & Tact\text{-}Peo & Ops\text{-}Peo \\ Strat\text{-}Tech & Tact\text{-}Tech & Ops\text{-}Tech \end{matrix}} \; v. \; \text{Project } B_{\text{Asset Type } y}^{\begin{matrix} Strat\text{-}Proc & Tact\text{-}Proc & Ops\text{-}Proc \\ Strat\text{-}Peo & Tact\text{-}Peo & Ops\text{-}Peo \\ Strat\text{-}Tech & Tact\text{-}Tech & Ops\text{-}Tech \end{matrix}}$$

[8] Assets are investment/project dependent and might include anything from buildings, to technology (e.g., hardware/software) or tools (i.e., physical, tangible things.)

Further, the ability to break down an Asset Type across the 9dimensions (Figure 11) allows you to compare across your *entire* portfolio, *regardless* of Asset Type, your overall process competencies, technical capabilities, and employee skills.

You can isolate any of the 9dimensions and evaluate your strengths and weaknesses, regardless of the Asset Type. You can more precisely conduct recruitment, technical training, or manage your outsourcing efforts. Dimensional views are one of the most powerful outcomes of the framework apart from risk management.

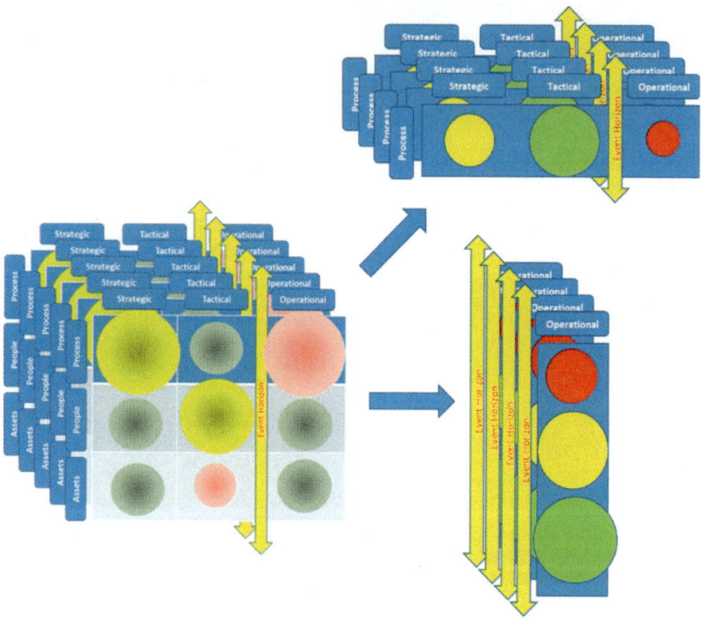

Figure 11 - 9dimensions Slices

Imagine drilling down from Asset Types to components, or moving from a component to all Asset Types which use it, to study enterprise-wide risk, resource usages, skill deficiencies, training needs, outsourcing options, or any other applicable analytics.

With standardized Asset Types and Components, you have complete visibility deep into or across all the work throughout the enterprise.

9DIMENSIONS QUESTIONS

In each of the dimensions, you are asking and answering questions (Figure 12) so you can best identify areas of *risk* and *return*, as relate to the specific intersection point or dimension.

For example, at the intersection of *Strategic* and *Process*, at the very least, you will ask and answer questions related to your Business Model and Business Process Model and changes you wish to make. You are evaluating the costs and benefits. Moreover, you are gauging potential effects on corporate objectives and Total Cost of Ownership (TCO.)

	Strategic	Tactical	Operational
Process	What processes or capabilities are we adding or modifying? And, Why?	Where and when do we want these processes and capabilities? Who should work on them and why?	How well are these processes working? Are they meeting objectives?
People	What people and with what skills do we need to support the processes and capabilities? And, why?	Where and when should these people be aligned within the org? Who and how should we bring them on board?	How well are the people adopting and working with the new capabilities? Are they keeping up? Do we need more training?
Assets	What tangible assets do we need to support the processes or capabilities? And, why?	Where and when will these assets reside? Who and how should we buy, build, or borrow these assets?	How well are our assets performing? Do we need to upgrade? Add on?

Figure 12 - 9dimensions Questions

Investments[9] supporting a global set of employees and customer base can be complex, with many failure points that need evaluation and risk mitigation.

[9] See the "Bonus 0 - Sample Asset Types" section for a sampling of components for a variety of different Asset Types / Investments.

■ ■ ■

It is in these framework-based Asset Types that lay the experiences of having done it many times over. We refine the precise set of components over many iterations, adjusting their half-life measures and risk profiles.

It is precisely because of these frameworks that consultancies are successful. They create best practices for whatever they do. They apply it. They refine and adjust it and, at each turn, they learn and adapt.

With our framework in mind, let's reflect on its usage by those who profit most from them: Consultancies.

Why Do Consultancies Succeed?

The consulting business can attribute its growth and success to many things but at its core, it is its ability to effectively and efficiently *duplicate* and *repurpose* its capabilities. They are methodical in everything that they do, from hiring, to training, to their work. It is their methodologies and processes, and their uniform adherence to that, which makes them succeed. We are only speaking about the top firms, those that have been around for decades, and who have a large global presence, and to all the smaller ones who have also templated their repeatable services.

When you call upon a consulting firm for a project, they rarely come to the table never having done dozens like it, or similar to it. It is rare for them to be novices[10]. They come to your aid with a portfolio of similar experiences. They come to you with detailed blueprints to do the job at hand. They manage their blueprint, their deliverables, and their processes across their framework.

▪ ▪ ▪

When they propose a piece of work. They outline the entire set of *components* required to get the job done.

[10] It is however, likely that the consultants who end up working on the project, after the proposal phase, are greenhorns. And that is your fault to the degree you allow it or pay for it. If you are hiring the greenhorns share the burden of their training by reducing the fees.

They do this for two reasons: It is *appropriate* and *profitable.*

- ***It is appropriate.*** For any project, they have to outline all the components necessary to succeed. The *components* list is something they have refined over years of doing that project (i.e., *Asset Type.*) Equally important, they are legally bound to point out all the components for success. Their credibility and knowledge base go hand in hand.
- ***It is profitable.*** Pointing out all the required components adds to the hourly billings and thus to the top and bottom lines.

■ ■ ■

They offer three kinds of service:

GOOD – CHEAP – FAST

(Pick Any Two)

GOOD Service CHEAP won't be FAST

GOOD Service FAST won't be CHEAP

FAST Service CHEAP won't be GOOD

Kidding aside, it seems as though on every proposal, there comes a point in the negotiations where the client asks, "*How can I reduce the cost?*"

This is common and understandable. However, more often than not it results in cutting costs in the wrong places. Consultancies often find themselves in the following dialog, with these common answers and discussion points:

"*You may cut the cost to zero, by not doing the project.*" A good starting point to put the fear of not doing anything in their minds.

"*Well, let's not go that far,*" they respond, concerned. "*What else can we do? Can we cut some work? Perhaps get rid of non-essential parts?*"

"*From our experience, all the components are essential to your success. We have done these dozens, if not hundreds, of times. We really can't get rid of any part."*

"Well, the price is too high. Maybe...," they pause.

"Maybe... we can do some of the work. After all, we have an entire IT department on-premise."

In order not to lose the project, consultants capitulate, knowing much of it will end up back in their lap, at higher revenues. *"I suppose that is one way to go. Which parts do you feel comfortable doing and wish to do?"*

Having examined the proposal at depth and having had discussions with their internal people, they offer suggestions, *"We believe we can do most if not all of sections 1-10, 20-33, and 47 to the end."*

The consultants reply knowing full well they will get all of it back and more in change orders, *"We really cannot let go of sections 20-33. We need control over that to succeed. However, we are fine with you doing the other sections as you suggest, but you must conform to our standards and methods so it all fits together nicely."*

"That would be no problem. So, how much will that save us?" they say happily, only thinking of the money they will save in the short run.

This conversation about pricing happens every time and is to the detriment of the project with these typical outcomes:

- More often, the client's lesser experienced people end up doing subpar work, or have a hard time conforming to the prescribed methodology or blueprint, requiring rework by consultants.
- The client forces the consultant to use less experienced staff at a reduced hourly rate to do the job resulting in more hours.
- The client fragments the project, bringing to the surface political strife and internal disagreements causing stoppages and bottlenecks.
- Parts of the project die in the process or never start.
- In the end, everyone works the *bill.* The client tries to reduce cost and the consultancy ties to manage their margins.

The blueprints and components that consultants offer are born out of experiences managing projects, investments of a particular Asset Type, and they have a deep understanding of risks as relate to the effort at hand. Stop haggling on the price as it comes back as change orders. Consultants are useful and a necessity. Mange them and the process well from the start.

Work the Process, not the Bill.

MANAGING CONSULTANTS

Consultants, third party experts, gurus, whatever you want to call them are an essential part of running your business. However, you need to manage them from day one to mitigate *risk* and maximize *returns.* There is no harm in taking charge. We mean *really* take charge and not accept that "you are in charge" because they say so in your weekly status meetings or invite you to fancy lunches filled with praise for your leadership "they pay for" but that show up buried somewhere within the monthly expense bill.

In most consulting projects, your only real power is choosing to pay the bill or not; unless you plan and contractually agree to a different model. Consultancies prefer you stay in your box and stay out of their way. You are to do as you're called on and not much more.

You're not In Charge,

unless you Take Charge.

No matter what they call you, or how often they meet with you, you are *not* in charge. It's a well-crafted and practiced illusion.

To be in charge, *institute your own* Delivery & Value Assurance processes. Fortunately, with a top tier consultancy, they do much of the work for you by virtue of how they do their contracts, Statements of Work (SOW), and responses to Requests for Proposals (RFP.)

Use their expertise to manage their work.

PROPOSAL PHASE

What they do…

When a company puts out an RFP, they get the early stages of a completed *framework*, including the requisite *components*. If the consultancy has done that work before, as they claim, the framework should be complete. In addition, that is how they price their projects.

What you should do…

For your part and as part of the review process, ask to see the exact templates corresponding to each component. (i.e., the deliverable template or a sample they are to follow.) You will use these to validate their work in the *Assurance Process*. If they have done the work, this should be easy and quick. If they have a hard time satisfying this request, most likely they have not done the work before. In either case, they may use the intellectual property and proprietary methodology card, which is valid to a point. Circumvent it through non-disclosure agreements, or pointing out that in all the projects done to date, having exposed the Intellectual Property (IP) to thousands of others, their business is not at risk from you, and that they have exposed the IP already, many times over.

What they do…

During the proposal phase, they will offer you many sample projects as references. Here is the truth. They definitely have done those projects somewhere on the globe, but most likely no one in the room has done those specific projects. In consulting, we call that the “Logo Page.”

For each project, some junior staff digs through the archives and finds representative projects that the consultancy has done. They then find the client logos, copy and paste that along with a blurb about the project, and slip the pages into the proposal. The logos are beautiful, and the blurbs are impressive. Sometimes, they even bring in the project manager from that reference project to help in the *sales process.*

What you should do…

You ask that the people who they bring on *be* the people who have done that specific *Asset Type*. Also, ask that all references in their proposal for previous work, be presented by the people who did the work so you can ask questions. Be comfortable that the consultancy and the consultant for which you are paying have done the work. That the people they are bringing on are those that did it firsthand, and that they are the ones who will *do* the project for you. This won't be easy.

There are several reasons they may not comply. For one, the people may not be at the firm or may be on another project or may be in another country or unwilling to commit. You should negotiate accordingly.

After all, you will train their staff, increasing your risk, and stretch the timeline otherwise.

CONTRACTING PHASE

What they do…

This is a tricky part but critical to success. The Statement of Work (SOW) and contracts are detailed, whether a time-and-materials or a fixed-priced contract. The contract's purpose is to detail each side's roles, contributions, responsibilities, and the mediation and reporting processes.

What you should do…

It is here where you need to take charge. You codify your role as

Delivery & Value Assurance managers in these contracts and SOWs. You may choose whatever language you wish, but it must entail:

- A Delivery & Value Assurance Process and Office.
- This office is permanent. It will be *your* command center.
- This office is *not* the program or project management office.
- You are *not* managing the project or its deliverables.
- You are managing risk and auditing components.
- You will manage and control this process, not the consultancy.
- Account and budget for their time (5± %.)
- Account and budget for your time (10± %.)

You can replace most status and project reporting costs with the assurance process. Fundamentally, status reporting is an absolute waste of time and money. They are biased, backwards looking, subjective, reactionary drivel slapped together to satisfy a reporting need.

Status Reports are Bulls#i!

ASSURANCE PROCESS

The process is methodical and akin to an audit, *an official inspection of an individual or organization's work, by an independent body*. Very much like an audit you are inspecting the *components*, re-evaluating *risk* and its effects on *returns* including costs.

Having established an Assurance Office, clarify contractually the steps within the process. As part of the baseline,

1. You must agree to every *component*, for which you are paying.
2. You must agree to its look and feel.
3. You must create Half-Life values.
4. You must create P(E) values.
5. You must create C(E) values.
6. You must understand the schedule.

7. You must have a process for approvals and disapprovals.
8. You must have a process to redo the disapprovals.
9. You must have a process to discount the cost for redoing components.

The Delivery & Value Assurance process is an audit of *components* where you are checking for *existence*: completeness, accessibility, and freshness. A component exists, if and only if ...

- It is *complete* in its content relative to the blueprint or template;
- It is *accessible* and known to everyone who needs it; **and**
- It is *up-to-date* and valid for current conditions.

On a weekly or bi-weekly basis, and randomly, you request a meeting at the Assurance Office where project managers bring the *components* for review. You and your review team, which comprises the assurance managers and Subject Matter Experts (SME), check for *existence*.

- For each item that *exists*, you subtract the incremental risk from the total investment risk. You then apply that new risk number to your investment return to establish a new baseline.
- Should items not pass the *existence* criteria or for those that expire based on their half-life value, you add the risks back into the overall risk pool. With risks added back in, calculate the new baseline and begin the process for rework and price adjustments.

Think of the Custom Software Development Asset Type[11] and its 58± components, the fully loaded framework, as you read the following section.

- Strategic-Process = 12 Components
- Strategic-People = 5 Components
- Strategic-Tech = 5 Components

---

[11] See "Bonus 0 - Sample Asset Types" for details.

- Tactical-Process = 11 Components
- Tactical-People = 9 Components
- Tactical-Tech = 10 Components
- Operational-Process = 8 Components
- Operational-People = 3 Components
- Operational-Tech = 5 Components

Having established your component level values (i.e., P(E), C(E), and Half-Life) you can create the worst-case scenario cost for the project. Given the estimated cost of "X" given to you by the consultancy, you apply your *Cost Multiplier* values, calculating a new higher cost "Y". The new and larger value "Y" is the worst-case scenario for that Asset Type. You should never exceed this number, and frankly, it is the number you should be comfortable with before you start the project, as it might *be* the final number.

Consultants manage their project (Figure 13) this way not with any malicious intent. They all do it this way. Remember, failure has a very strong gravitational pull, and a consultancy makes more money the longer it takes. There is no incentive to fight the gravitational pull.

Figure 13 - Consulting Pricing Model

The way you should manage (Figure 14) is to start from the failure side, with the worst-case scenario, with all cost multipliers applied, and work your way to the proposed original value with a systematic *Delivery & Value Assurance* process.

Figure 14 - Your Pricing Model

Focus on the components with the highest risk profiles, as they will have the costliest effects. Prioritize the assurance process so you spend

50% on the top third, 33% on the middle, and 17% on the lowest third. This approach does not guarantee that you will end up at the original proposed lower cost of X, but it will most definitely not be the higher Y cost and if you're good at the assurance process, it will be a far closer number to X than to Y.

An extreme side benefit is that you are proactively fighting the gravitational pull, moving away from failure and pushing the consultancy towards their original proposed cost of X. Also, this approach focuses your attention on the work and the process, not the bill. But the result is a reduced project cost.

WIP PHASE

Don't use the Assurance Process to manage the project or for creating components and deliverables. The purpose behind the process is to manage *risks* and *returns*. The process helps with a top-down, forward-looking, preventative, unbiased, objective view of the investment, allowing for *risk* mitigation as early as possible. Early risk mitigation minimizes costs and maximizes returns – a continuous process that goes on throughout the investment's life cycle.

By having a strong assurance process in place and having contractually agreed to it with the consultancy, you are compelling them to focus on doing the job effectively and accurately to start.

It's a Win-Win all around.

We implemented the assurance process at many companies and found a much higher success rate in audited projects. Moreover, we kept project costs under control, and we had *no* surprises.

With an established assurance process, you can calculate failure rates and TCO before you spend much time or money. As you refine your capabilities, and develop your knowledge base, you can gain insights into investments before you spend *any* money.

Become a Consultancy

This is not to promote changing anything about your business, but to apply the best features of a consultancy to the way you *manage* your investments.

A consultancy succeeds because it is a business and runs the work that it does as a business. It knows it will do the same work repeatedly and thus creates reusable templates, processes, methods, tools, and capabilities further supported by a centrally maintained and globally accessible knowledge base. It is after all a margins business. As costs and related billing rates increase annually, the only way to increase margins is through efficiency and optimization.

Not that you should spend massive amounts of money duplicating their infrastructure and capability. However, for the work that you do regularly, attempt to change core abilities to match those of the best in the field.

INVESTMENT SELECTION AND SETUP

We have sat on hundreds of investment and project selection meetings and have never left filled with joy at how well it ran. It has often been a disappointment to see how, over decades in the field, nothing much has changed.

At the highest levels, every company sets objectives it tries to achieve annually. In consultancies it is simple and may include increasing top line revenue by 20% and increasing margins by 3%. Given the primary set of objectives, each business division *subscribes* to a share of that. The Outsourcing Group might subscribe to increase 15% of the 20% top line revenue objective and to 5% of the 3% margin requirements. So goes the annual objectives and subscriptions course for each business unit.

In corporations, a similar event occurs. Where the upper echelons come up with annual corporate objectives, around ten to fifteen of them. They are further broken down into subsets of objectives.

Where each objective is (theoretically):

1. ***Precise*** - A specific objective should detail where you want to arrive, unequivocally.
2. ***Quantifiable*** - It must be measurable.
3. ***Attainable*** - It must be believable.
4. ***Pertinent*** - It must link to the company's strategy.
5. ***Temporal*** - It must be timely.

And, they typically fall into one of these categories.

- Financial, e.g.,

  Increase Top Line Revenue, Increase Margins, Decrease Costs, Increase Stock Prices, Increase Dividends
- Customer, e.g.,

  Increase Market Share, Increase Customer Return Rates, Increase Customer Satisfaction Rates, Increase Customer Share of Wallet, Increase Customer Touch Points, Increase New Customers, Improve Customer Retention
- Internal, e.g.,

  Increase R&D, Grow Sales by New Products, Optimize and Streamline Processes, Reduce Headcount, Reduce Wastage, Improve Workforce Safety, Improve Workforce Productivity, Reduce Energy Consumption, Capitalize on Facilities, Reduce Error Rates
- Regulatory, e.g.,

Ensure Compliance, Increase Reporting and Transparency, Increase Community Outreach

- Training and Growth, e.g.,
  Improve technical and Analytical Skills, Improve Certain Skills, Improve Culture, Improve Collaboration, Improve Workforce Retention

▪ ▪ ▪

With *objectives* selected and quantified, along with underlying business unit objectives, every Investment / Asset Type must *subscribe* to at least one objective. For each, the investment should quantify their contributions. For example, if the investment claims it can increase top line revenue, it must take the objective (e.g., Increase Revenue By 5% globally) and stake a claim as to how much of it will be *theirs* (e.g., 10% of 5%, or 0.5% of total increases will be attributed to them.)

If you cannot subscribe to any objective in a quantifiable way, do not proceed. You are wasting your money.

Similarly, if the full amount has been subscribed to (i.e., all 5% has been staked out by other investments), be cautious about adding more because you may waste resources. Although some over-subscription is reasonable as not all projects come through on their promises, strive to limit it.

In our audits and portfolio assessments, 68% could not subscribe to a single corporate objective, in any meaningful or quantifiable way.

PROCESS CHANGES

In a consultancy, they centralize all of their processes in some fashion. At any point, they know the state of every existing and potential client. They know where every consultant is and what they're working on. They know their cash flows intimately. They know where each project stands, and which might get them in trouble.

You should at the very least have a centralized and enterprise-wide *Delivery & Value Assurance* capability, with a broad reach. It is in this centralized knowledge base where you can garner the values of reusability, the most up-to-date views of risk, the most up-to-date understanding of how to measure your risks, and the best way to maintain a top-down view and control of all investments. You should be the *clearinghouse* for all Asset Types.

Your charter should be such that you…

- Review each investment to make sure it is subscribing to one or more objectives, while minimizing over-subscriptions.
- You are not program managers.
- You are not project managers.
- You are not to evaluate projects beyond ascertaining *risks*.
- You are keepers of the *framework*.
- You are keepers of *Asset Types*, their structure, and *components*.
- You have the best in methods, templates, and examples to share, for as many of the *Asset Types* and *components* as possible. This will evolve, with the added benefit that over time you become more proficient in gauging risk for each *component*.
- You are the mediators of *risk* across the entire enterprise.

HIRING AND TRAINING CHANGES

As time progresses and as your Assurance Office grows its knowledge base, you will become the source for discovering resource and skill deficiencies. Your company's ability to deliver on components will be clear and you can gauge best where you are short in certain capabilities that can best be recharged by *training*, *recruiting*, or *outsourcing*.

Use your insights into the Asset Types you've implemented and that you will implement, and the underlying Components to determine:

1. How well did we do on delivering prior components?
    a. Did we do it by ourselves?
    b. Did we do it with help from others?
    c. At what costs?
2. Can we deliver on the components going forward?
    a. If not, can we train, hire, or outsource to meet the deficiencies? At what cost?
    b. Can we replace the components with other equivalent components with which we are well versed, and can deliver?
    c. Can we replace the Asset Type with another? And, can we deliver that?

Train, hire, and outsource

based on the above analysis.

Become True Portfolio Managers

True Portfolio Management (TPM) differs from *Project Portfolio Management* (PPM). Having developed one of the very first applications that does portfolio management for pension and mutual funds as well as having developed one of the first TPM SAAS solutions for projects, the differences are stark.

PPM

"A senior leadership discipline that drives strategic execution and maximizes business value delivery through the selection, optimization, and oversight of project investments which align to business goals and strategies." WikiPedia.org

PPM is what most people in the project and program management world know best, *theoretically* offering:

- Portfolio planning
- Investment ranking
- Portfolio balancing
- Resource planning
- Master scheduling

Best used for circumstances where

- Investments are mission critical
- Investments span more than one business unit
- Investments are large

Having looked at many PPM tools and dozens of implementations, and having audited their usages, we can say emphatically they are not Portfolio Management in any true sense of the term. They are useful, valuable, and have a place. However, they are nothing more than *inventory management* tools. They are Project Management tools on steroids. A place to keep track of the projects and resources on which an enterprise is spending money. It is a place to aggregate status reports and tabulate subjective risk measures. It is a place where you track cash outflows and expenses. Granted, you do make portfolio type decisions such as selecting, launching and terminating projects, analyzing risk, and planning resource allocations. In addition, you might even call projects "assets", and may even have the concept of Asset Types. In all, they've borrowed many of the terms but are *not* conducting true portfolio management.

Don't get us wrong, we think inventory management is necessary but insufficient.

Calling a process by a different name

does not make it so.

You are not portfolio managers.

TPM

True Portfolio Management is the process of managing stocks, bonds, etc., within a fund, where risk and returns are quantifiable to the extreme, and where you measure, track, compare, and correlate every investment, all of which feed into a balancing process, with a rinse and repeat feature.

"[True] Portfolio Management is the art

and science of making decisions about

investment mix and policy, matching investments to objectives, asset allocation for individuals and institutions, and balancing risk against performance,"

InvestOpedia.com

PPM v. TPM

As mentioned earlier, the differences are stark although the terms are similar.

Risk Differences…

- In PPM, risks are aggregated status reports and red-yellow-green switches based on a program or project manager's *views*, which are highly subjective, backwards looking, reactive, and repair-oriented.
- In TPM, risks are highly quantifiable measures based on components that make up a specific investment. They are forward looking, objective, quantifiable, and allow for risk mitigation before it materializes.

Relationship Differences…

- In PPM, there does not exist a quantifiable correlative analysis on investments within a portfolio. There is no methodical way to analyze the effects of one investment on all other investments in a portfolio. There are schedule and resource conflicts, but they are bitwise comparisons at best.
- In TPM, every single investment is correlated to every single other investment in that portfolio. Every investment's effects on every other investment is known, at any point in time.

Examining relationships is critical in balancing a portfolio. In PPM there is no domino or cascade analysis, making the balancing process of limited use.

Returns Differences…

- In PPM, rarely do you do *returns management* in its true sense. You spend a great deal of time tracking costs and expenses, but hardly do you track the cash inflows, or effects on companywide financial ratios or objectives. There is not even a subscription model in place to track what the investments are supposed to offer back to the company and on what basis.
- In TPM, returns management is the core capability. The entire process undertakes a concrete ability to track cash outflows against returns in the form of appreciation and dividends. Every dollar correlates directly to a value or lack thereof, and that supports the balancing process.

INCORPORATE TPM IN PPM

You are thinking it is impossible to apply True Portfolio Management to enterprise investments. We are here to say you are wrong, and it has and can be done. Not only that, but the very first Project Portfolio Management SAAS Software ever written was exactly that, a true portfolio management capability applied to investments companies make in their people, process, and assets/technology.

However, it is difficult to incorporate the best of TPM into existing PPM implementations, but you can establish certain capabilities as procedural side features to enhance what you may already have.

The Case for Risk…

Every PPM implementation has a way to manage risk, but you can substantially enhance the collection of inputs, for the risk measure, with the *Delivery & Value Assurance* process described earlier. Instead of trusting project managers with their red-yellow-green traffic light updates, conduct assurance reviews and input *those* results into the PPM tool.

The Case for Relationships...

Most PPM tools have resource-tracking features focused on employees or contractors as part of the project billing and cost allocation features, some may even manage resources in the form of space, computing time, and other hard asset usages. Enhance this with the results of the assurance process for any one investment, with how it relates to all other investments in that portfolio.

The Case for Returns...

In the Assurance Office and as part of the investment selection process, institute a companywide subscription model whereby investments have to provide what they propose to offer back to the company through effecting objectives[12].

They must make evident their contributions back to the enterprise.

Wrap your Assurance Process around your PPM tool, and thereby Profit.

[12] These objectives are more in line with Objectives and Key Results (OKR) and not Key Performance Indicators (KPI). OKRs are a metric that outline company or team "objectives" along with the measurable "key results" that define the achievement of those objectives. You are subscribing to a portion of those “key results” as *your* responsibility.

Integrate Your Talent

Considering talent beyond where they're working can be consequential in so many ways. The one thing that PPM does well is the management of employees for cost allocation and project billing. There is a concerted effort to know where they are and what they are working on, but only as it applies to a project in the PPM system. A good start, but there is more to do.

The largest contributors to *risk* are people. More specifically, their deficiencies as relate to *components* of an Asset Type. The components that are part and parcel of an investment and that ask, analyze, and answer the questions required for successfully moving forward at every step, are created by people. Thus, deficiencies in components tie directly to deficiencies in the people creating them. Not all deficiencies are skills related. Some tie to a lack of time, a lack of interest, or in a worst-case, malicious intent.

In all cases, it is important to know what *roles* and *skills* correlate to what *components*, and ultimately to which specific people in every investment. Manage your people beyond their time. Manage and enhance their skills. You will end up more successful and with happier employees. Do this through training and rotating them through different projects.

CAPABILITY MAPPING

To boost your control over *risk* while managing your resources beyond job titles, it is well worth mapping your capabilities[13] to roles and to components (Figure 15). When you assign employees to investments, do so by their role not their title, where every employee may be qualified in more than one role. A very common practice in all consultancies.

As you go through your assurance processes, you can directly tie component *risk* to specific roles, which helps you determine any deficiencies you may have, that you can remedy through training, hiring, or outsourcing. Over time, you can plan your resource needs better based directly on the Asset Types in which you foresee making investments. You can plan your training programs and hiring programs. When and if you outsource your work, you can better manage areas that you can supplement best and at the lowest cost.

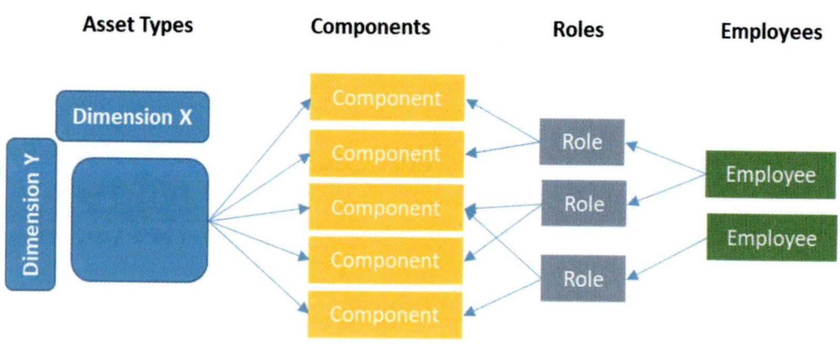

Figure 15 - Capability Mapping

[13] See "Bonus I - Capability Mapping" for more details.

The Process Recapitulated

Manage investments you make in your people, process, and assets/technologies as you would any investment. Implement an assurance process where you manage your investment risks and returns before and after the event horizon, and throughout its life cycle, from cradle to grave. And, manage your investments as true portfolio managers.

THE BASELINE

Start by creating reusable ***Asset Types*** to define your investments. These are reusable investment ***frameworks***.

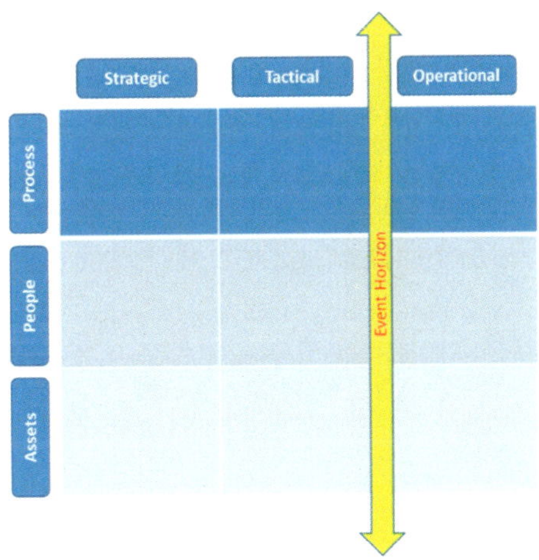

The framework may include few or many dimensions. We recommend using the nine dimensions of *Strategy*, *Tactical*, and *Operational* against *People*, *Process*, and *Assets*[14].

[14] Where assets include technology, tools, capital assets, etc.

For each of the *Asset Types*, create and outline a detailed list of *components* that define that investment in its entirety (Figure 16).

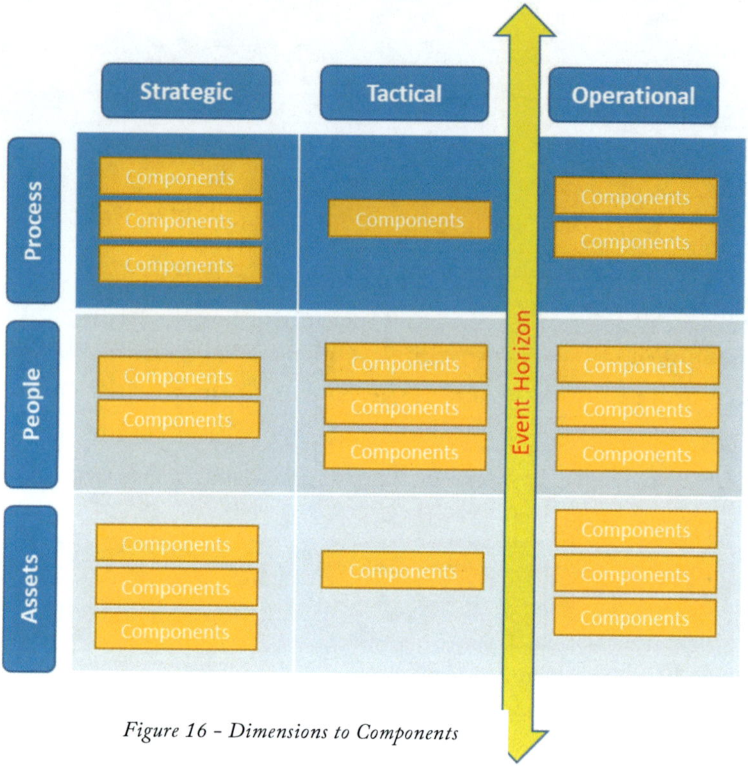

Figure 16 - Dimensions to Components

For each component, create a blueprint, a method for creation, and if possible best practices samples (Figure 17).

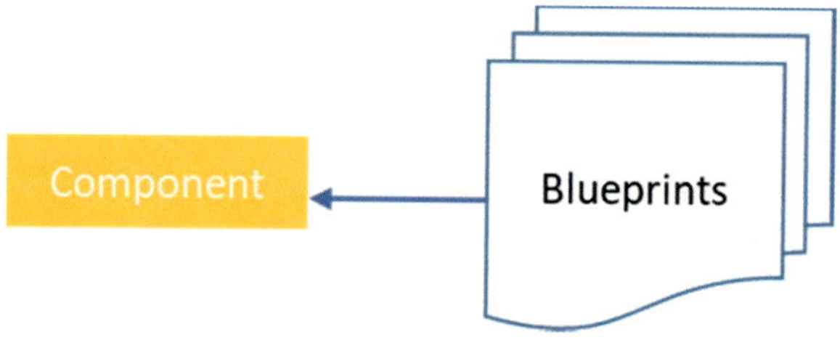

Figure 17 - Component to Blueprints

Map each component to roles within your enterprise (Figure 18).

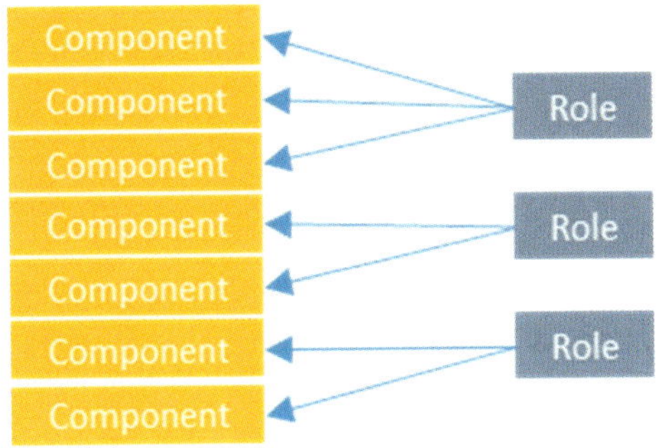

Figure 18 - Components to Roles

Map employees to roles (Figure 19).

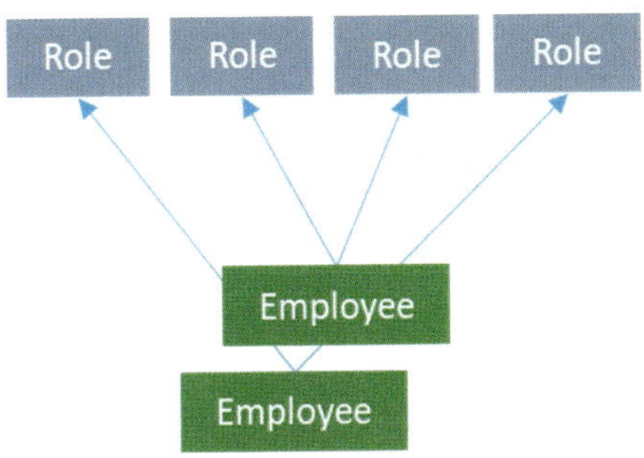

Figure 19 - Employees to Roles

Later in this chapter we'll present the Entity Relationship Model (ERM) for this process, but for now, remember this:

- Asset Types have one or more dimensions, each with one or more components, each component is created by a role that is assigned to an employee.
- Therefore, you can draw a line:
- from asset type to
- component to
- role to
- employee and back.

INVESTMENT SELECTION

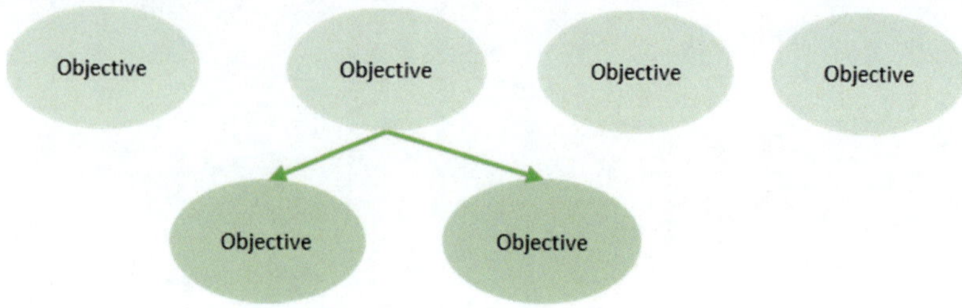

Figure 20 - Objectives

Before any investment selection, collect and quantify all the enterprise objectives and breakdown further if possible (Figure 20). For each investment in a particular Asset Type, *subscribe* to one or more objectives (Figure 21).

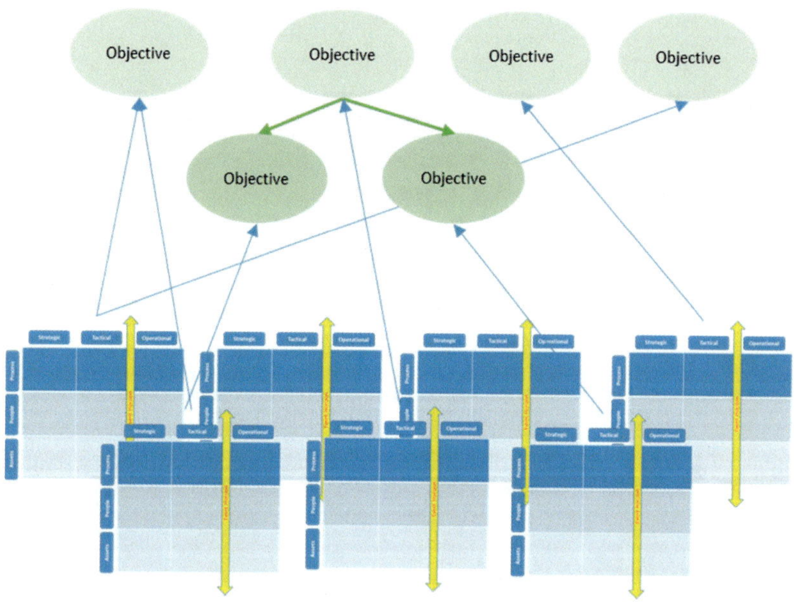

Figure 21 - Objectives to Investments

If an investment cannot subscribe to any objectives in a measurable and substantive manner, and cannot quantify a payback, then eliminate the investment. Eliminate over-subscribing to specific objectives.

THE ASSURANCE PROCESS

Setup an enterprise-wide Assurance Office, with a broad mandate to conduct both *Delivery* & *Value Assurance*.

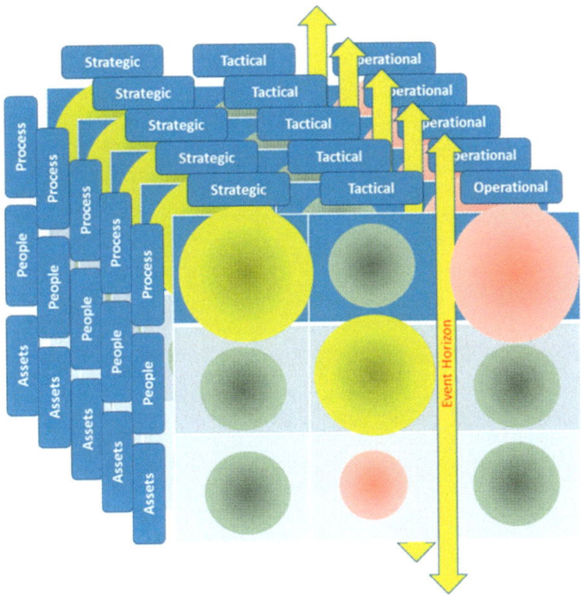

Figure 22 - Investment Risk View

- *Delivery Assurance* - assuring the delivery of stated requirements on time. In short, the study of risk and failure points on schedules, and their mitigation.
- **Value Assurance** - assuring the achievement of financial value to the enterprise top and bottom lines. In short, the analysis of risk's effects on returns, and its mitigation.

The process should incorporate evaluating components for *existence* against the predefined Asset Type, its underlying components list and associated templates or approved samples. Summarize the incremental risk at every dimension (Figure 22) resulting in a scaled heat map.

Evaluate relationship risks between investments within a portfolio (Figure 23). This may include financial consequences (e.g., budget constraints, etc.) as well as resource consequences (e.g., hardware and network bandwidth requirements, skills usage, etc.)

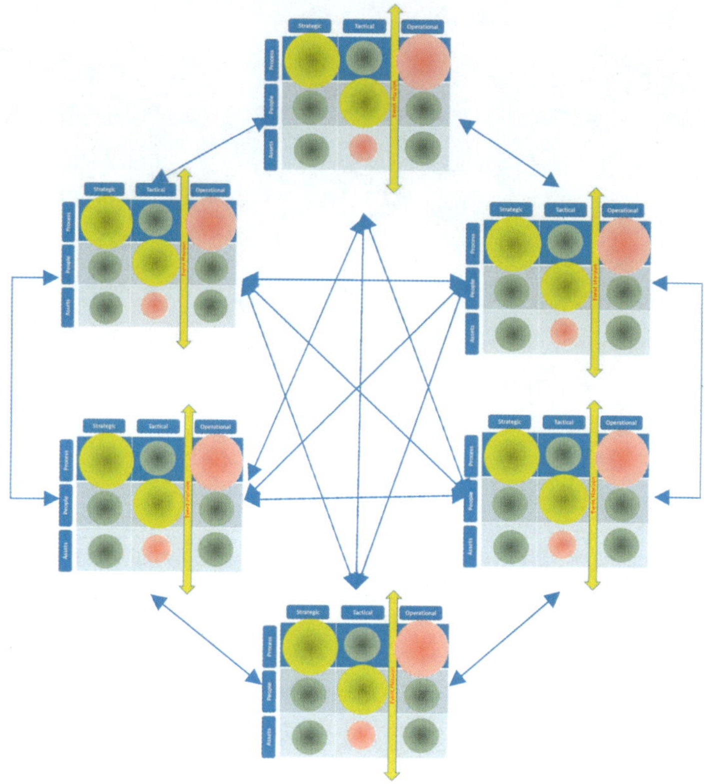

Figure 23 - Portfolio of Projects

Evaluate risk by role and named employee (Figure 24).

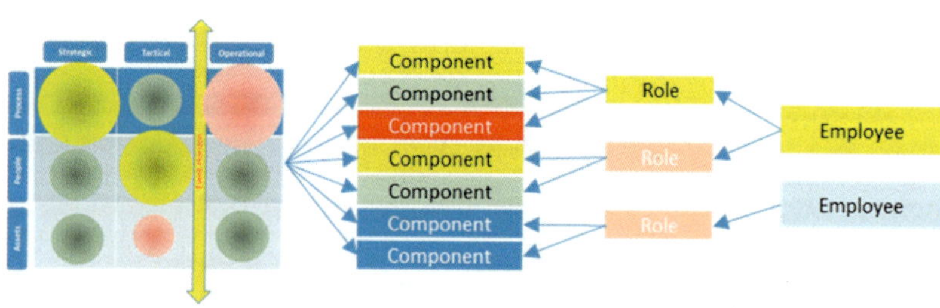

Figure 24 - Risk by Components, Roles, and Employees

PORTFOLIO BALANCING

Portfolio balancing (Figure 25) is the proactive act of elimination, addition, and modification of investments within a portfolio. With investments made in your people, processes, and assets, it may include outright elimination (blackout), contraction, or expansion e.g., in resources, funding, etc., or adding new investments, keeping in mind all the previous assurance steps.

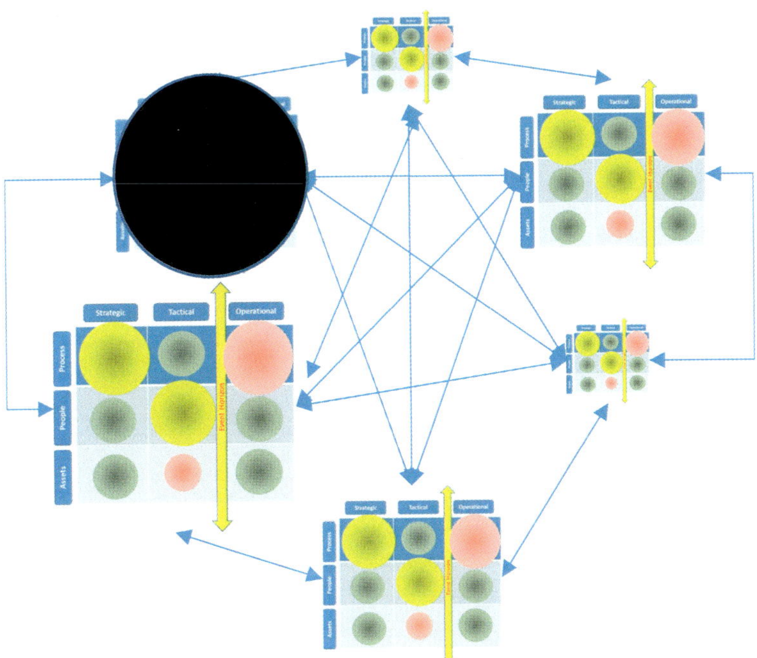

Figure 25 - Portfolio Balancing

TERMS AND DEFINITIONS

From the top…

- *Asset Type* - an investment's reusable *framework.*
- *Framework* - a collection of two or more dimensions, each consisting of *components* that define elements of an investment whose successful completion helps minimize *risk* and maximize *returns.*
- *Risk* - a quantifiable value based on the probability of an event occurring (uncertainty) multiplied by the cost associated with the event (exposure.)
- *Return* - a quantifiable value associated with an investment, which diminishes as risk values increase.
- *Half-Life* - the expiration time for *components* within a *framework,* upon which there is an automatic re-introduction of incremental *risk* back into the investment's total *risk.*
- *Delivery Assurance* - assuring the delivery of stated requirements on time and within budget. In short, the study of risk and failure points.
- *Value Assurance* - assuring the achievement of financial value to the enterprise top and bottom lines. In short, the analysis of *risk's* effects on *returns.*
- *Portfolio Balancing* - proactively eliminating, adding, and modifying investments within a portfolio, utilizing risk and return measures as your input.

THE PROCESS DATA MODEL

In Brief …

- *Portfolios* include *Projects*, which are based on standardized *Asset Types*, which are composed of *Components*.
- *Employees*, in their *Roles*, complete (deliver) *Components*.
- Conduct the Delivery and Value Assurance process on Portfolios, Projects, Asset Types, and their Components.
- *Recruit and Train Employees* to satisfy *Roles*, which are responsible for *Components*.
- Conduct *Risk and Returns Management* across the entire spectrum.

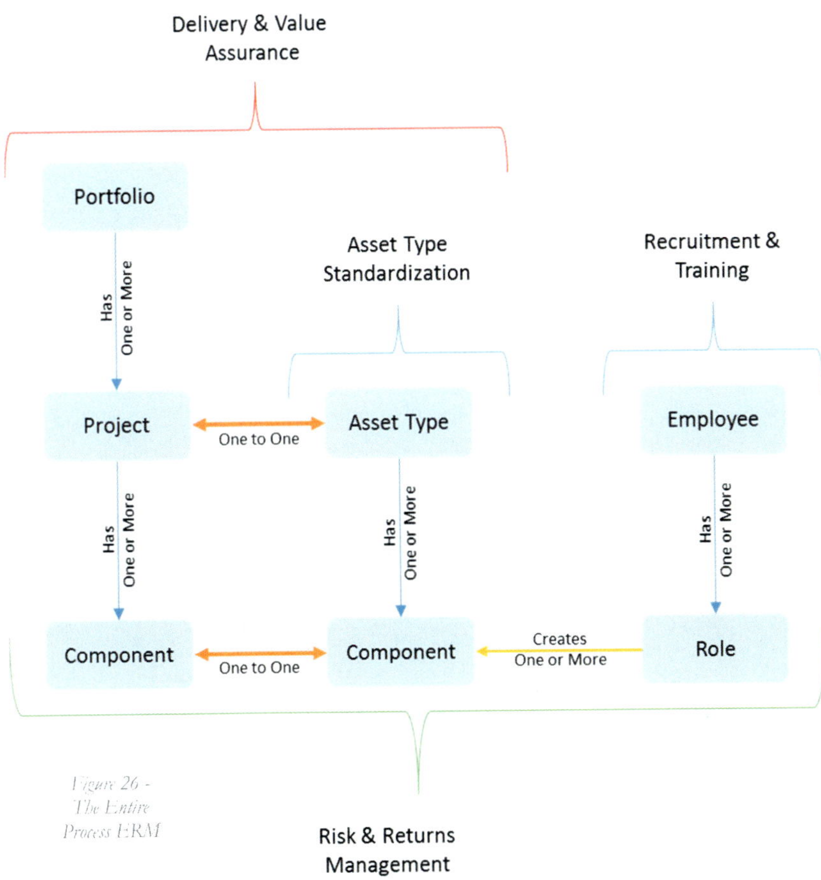

Figure 26 - The Entire Process ERM

IN LAYMEN'S TERMS

If someone comes to you with a $100 project with five components and some end-result, do the following:

1. Check which objectives they are to satisfy with their end-results and by how much.
    a. If none. Don't proceed.
    b. Otherwise, check to see if it's already being done.
2. Apply component deficiency cost multipliers to the $100 to calculate worst-case cost (e.g., $500)
    a. If you're comfortable with $500 and #1 still applies, proceed.
    b. If you're not comfortable, make sure you can deliver on the components in your existing condition thus reducing the $500 and that #1 still applies.
    c. Otherwise, don't proceed.
3. Check on projects affected by you or that affect you.
    a. If everyone's comfortable, proceed.
4. Conduct your assurance process throughout the life cycle.
    a. Don't forget to cut your losses at any point.

INFORMATION ECHOING

Many of the tools out in the market may claim to enable and support portfolio management, but most of these solutions will prove disappointing. The reason for this is in their foundation and origin. The historical origins of these vendors has typically been on singular project management solutions and therefore, the bottom-up capturing and reporting of granular and highly subjective data elements. The only difference now is they've aggregated and summarized this data from vast numbers of user and slapped a portfolio management label on it for credibility. We call this form of reporting *information echoing* and it is not at all reflective of true investment management and assurance as we've tried to explain here.

The key to getting even minimally useful results from their

approach is ensuring three things companies have little control over: *adherence*, *timeliness*, and *truthfulness*. These subjective factors can vary from day to day, person to person, and are highly susceptible to both corporate politics and personal moods. Many of these solutions support choosing investments in the same democratic manner as a group might choose pizza toppings. These approaches have not lifted low success rates for single projects. They certainly haven't helped when aggregated together in a multi-project management system, and they won't work as claimed for true portfolio management.

All these information echoing approaches share a universal trait. They assume absolute success for every investment from the very beginning. Then, each investment inevitably works its way toward *failure* as accruing data and opinions e.g., status reports or quarterly business reviews, indicate problems. You're guaranteed to be behind in formulating a response because you're relying on chronically belated, backward-looking, and imprecise information. Worst of all, with these aggregation tools, bad decisions are being made faster, at levels farther removed from the real truth, and therefore undertaken with a greater sense of false confidence.

IMMUNIZE YOUR INVESTMENTS FROM FAILURE

Investments in processes, people and physical assets are a mainstay of your growth strategy. In challenging economic or competitive times, investment assurance is crucial. The patented *Delivery and Value Assurance* methods described herein begin by recognizing there is a baseline probability of failure for each investment type. However, by applying these defined assurance processes, you can proactively and progressively guide each investment to conclusive success. This approach is based on fully understanding your business objectives and your organization's capability to deliver on those investments. True investment assurance uses a consistent, comparative underlying framework, along with proven practices in program and project management, oversight, independent validation and verification, and financial investment management adapted for a project environment.

Only in this manner may your company objectively and measurably minimize risks, optimize relationships between investments, and maximize returns from each one of them, thereby assuring all your investments are effective at …

Escaping

the gravitational

pull of failure.

Bonus 0 | Sample Asset Types

Here are a sample of Asset Types[15] we have worked on, for which we have created the 9dimensions framework, and to which we have applied the *Delivery & Value Assurance* process.

- Anti-Money Laundering
- Application Outsourcing (AO) Migration
- AO: Service Provider
- AO: Application Development
- AO: Application Development/Management
- AO: Application Management
- AO: Design, Build, Run
- Basel II Services
- Business Process Optimization (BPO) Migration
- BPO: Accounts Payable and Receivable
- BPO: Call Center
- BPO: Contract Management
- BPO: Fixed Asset Management
- BPO: GL Accounting

[15] Items in red are expanded later in the bonus section.

- BPO: HR
- BPO: Invoicing and Collections
- BPO: Procurement - Order Expediting
- BPO: Procurement - Order Processing
- BPO: Procurement - Spend Data Management
- BPO: Project Accounting
- BPO: Vendor Management
- Business Continuity
- Business Process Re-Engineering (large scale)
- Business Project Services
- Business Systems Design
- Communications Development
- Corporate Security
- Custom Off the Shelf (COTS) Software Package Deployment
- COTS: Package Design and Prototyping
- COTS: Package Evaluation and Selection
- COTS: Package System Design
- COTS: Package Testing/Piloting
- COTS: Package Upgrade
- Credit Risk Management
- Custom Software Development (large scale)
- Custom Application Retrofitting
- Education Development
- Enterprise (Business Area) Architecture
- Enterprise Risk Management
- Enterprise Transformation
- Financial Investigations

- Large-Scale System Services Procurement
- Litigation Readiness
- Merger or Acquisition
- Operational Resilience
- Organizational Model Analysis and Design
- Organizational Model Transition
- Revenue Optimization
- Sarbanes-Oxley Compliance
- Spend Risk [Non-Core]
- Staff Planning and Development
- Staff Transition
- Supply Chain Risk
- Technical Infrastructure Acquisition & Deployment
- Technical Infrastructure Analysis & Design
- Treasury Risk Management

SAMPLE COMPONENTS

CUSTOM SOFTWARE DEVELOPMENT (LARGE SCALE)

The following is a complete *components* list for the *Asset Type* broken down by dimensions.

Strategic | Process Components

Data Model Views and Flows ■ Logical Business Process Hierarchy, Definitions and Events ■ Conceptual Flow Diagrams ■ Proposed Business Change Reports ■ Value Chain Analysis ■ Conceptual Business Process Hierarchy ■ Business Process Principles, Constraints & Assumptions ■ Process Relationship Map ■ Customer & User Needs / Process Matrix ■ Process / Function Map, Criticality Map & Flow Diagram ■ Conceptual Business Event & Results Definitions ■ Business Process Value and Performance Models

Strategic | People Components

Organizational Transition Plan ■ Stakeholder Model ■ Acceptance Plan for Program Management ■ Stakeholder Communication and Enrollment Plan ■ Organizational Change Measurement Plan

Strategic | Asset/Technology Components

Technology Model View ■ Procurement Work Products ■ Legacy Transformation Strategy ■ Application Portfolio Assessment ■ Application Architecture

Tactical | Process Components

Program Completion Plan ■ Other Supporting Plans for Program Management ■ Program Guidelines ■ Program Management Plan ■ Program Dependencies ■ Program-Critical Interface List ■ Test Plans and Materials ■ Template Site Deployment Plan ■ Business Transformation Plan ■ Business Transformation Model ■ Business Process Transformation Model ■ Vendor Evaluation and Management Plan

Tactical | People Components

Location Model View ■ Organization Model View ■ Transition Model ■ Organizational Change Plan ■ Other Organizational Reports ■ Program Management Organization ■ Review and Inspection Materials ■ Staff Management Work Products ■ Staffing Plans

Tactical | Asset/Technology Components

Application Model View ■ Development Products and Life-Cycle Reports ■ Monitoring and Tracking ■ Other (Special Purpose) Development Plans ■ Other Feasibility and Analysis Reports

Prototypes ■ System Requirements Model ■ Application Transformation Model ■ Technology Transformation Model ■ System Engineering Model View ■ Development Products

Operational | Process Components

Issue Management ■ Document Management ■ Configuration Management ■ Enterprise Transformation Plans ■ Release Plans ■ Deployment Site Plans ■ Other Operational and Post-Transition Reports ■ Disaster Recovery and Contingency Plans

Operational | People Components

Data Transformation Model ■ Organizational Change Unit Review Plan ■ On-Duty List

Operational | Asset/Technology Components

Operations System Support Plan ■ Quality Management Work Products ■ Risk Management Work Products ■ Physical Application Transformation ■ Existing Systems Documentation

MORE COMPONENTS

Components (x,y)[16] for more of the *Asset Types* listed earlier.

BUSINESS PROCESS RE-ENGINEERING (LARGE SCALE)

Conceptual Flow Diagrams (1,1)
Proposed Business Change Reports (1,1)
Value Chain Analysis (1,1)
Conceptual Business Process Hierarchy (1,1)
Business Process Principles, Constraints & Assumptions (1,1)
Process Relationship Map - Present State (1,1)
Process/Function Map, Criticality Map & Flow Diagram (1,1)
Conceptual Business Event & Results Definitions (1,1)
Business Process Value and Performance Models (1,1)
Customer & User Needs / Process Matrix (1,1)
Stakeholder Communication and Enrollment Plan (1,2)
Organizational Change Measurement Plan (1,2)
Organizational Transition Plan (1,2)
Stakeholder Model (1,2)
Acceptance Plan for Program Management (1,2)
Technology Model View (1,3)
Information Technology Strategic Plan (1,3)
Application Portfolio Assessment (1,3)
Other Supporting Plans for Program Management (2,1)
Location Model View (2,2)
Organization Model View (2,2)
Transition Model (2,2)
Organizational Change Plan (2,2)
Other Organizational Reports (2,2)
Program Management Organization (2,2)
Review and Inspection Materials (2,2)
Staff Management Work Products (2,2)
Staffing Plans (2,2)
Development Products (2,3)
Development Life Cycle Reports (2,3)
Monitoring and Tracking (2,3)
Other (Special Purpose) Development Plans (2,3)
Other Feasibility and Analysis Reports (2,3)
Application Transformation Model (2,3)
Technology Transformation Model (2,3)
Application Model View (2,3)
Configuration Management (3,1)
Enterprise Transformation Plans (3,1)
Release Plans (3,1)
Deployment Site Plans (3,1)
Other Operational and Post-Transition Reports (3,1)
Disaster Recovery and Contingency

16 X is 1 = Strategic, 2 = Tactical, or 3 = Operational;
Y is 1 = Process, 2 = People, or 3 = Assets/Technology

Legacy Transformation Strategy (1,3)
Vendor Evaluation and Management Plan (2,1)
Program Dependencies (2,1)
Test Plans and Materials (2,1)
Business Transformation Plan (2,1)
Business Transformation Model (2,1)
Program Management Plan (2,1)
Program Guidelines (2,1)
Program Completion Plan (2,1)
Template Site Deployment Plan (2,1)
Plans (3,1)
Document Management (3,1)
Organizational Change Unit Review Plan (3,2)
Data Transformation Model (3,2)
Existing Systems Documentation (3,3)
Operations System Support Plan (3,3)
Quality Management Work Products (3,3)
Risk Management Work Products (3,3)

BUSINESS SYSTEM DESIGN

Data Model Views, Flows, et al. (1,1)
Logical Business Process Hierarchy, Definitions & Events (1,1)
Conceptual Flow Diagrams (1,1)
Conceptual Business Process Hierarchy (1,1)
Proposed Business Change Reports (1,1)
Value Chain Analysis (1,1)
Business Process Principles, Constraints & Assumptions (1,1)
Process Relationship Map - Present State (1,1)
Customer & User Needs / Process Matrix (1,1)
Process / Function Map, Criticality Map & Flow Diagram (1,1)
Conceptual Business Event & Results Definitions (1,1)
Business Process Value and Performance Models (1,1)
Organizational Transition Plan (1,2)
Stakeholder Model (1,2)
Acceptance Plan for Program Management (1,2)
Procurement Work Products (1,3)
Technology Model View (1,3)
Information Technology Strategic Plan (1,3)
Legacy Transformation Strategy (1,3)
Business Transformation Plan (2,1)
Management (2,1)
Program Management Plan (2,1)
Program Dependencies (2,1)
Program Completion Plan (2,1)
Other Supporting Plans for Program Management (2,1)
Project Management Plan (2,1)
Program Guidelines (2,1)
Location Model View (2,2)
Organization Model View (2,2)
Transition Model (2,2)
Organizational Change Plan (2,2)
Other Organizational Reports (2,2)
Program Management Organization (2,2)
Review and Inspection Materials (2,2)
Staffing Plans (2,2)
Development Products (2,3)
Development Life Cycle Reports (2,3)
Monitoring and Tracking (2,3)
Other (Special Purpose) Development Plans (2,3)
Other Feasibility and Analysis Reports (2,3)
System Requirements Model (2,3)
Application Model View (2,3)
System Engineering Model View (2,3)
Application Transformation Model (2,3)
Technology Transformation Model (2,3)
Enterprise Transformation Plans (3,1)

Business Transformation Model (2,1)
Business Process Transformation Model (2,1)
Test Plans and Materials (2,1)
Other Supporting Plans for Project
Document Management (3,1)
Issue Management (3,1)
Data Transformation Model (3,2)
Operations System Support Plan (3,3)

STAFF PLANNING AND DEVELOPMENT

Process Relationship Map - Present State (1,1)
Customer & User Needs / Process Matrix (1,1)
Process/Function Map, Criticality Map & Flow Diagram (1,1)
Business Process Value and Performance Models (1,1)
Stakeholder Communication and Enrollment Plan (1,2)
Stakeholder Model (1,2)
Procurement Work Products (1,3)
Application Portfolio Assessment (1,3)
Legacy Transformation Strategy (1,3)
Information Technology Strategic Plan (1,3)
Vendor Evaluation and Management Plan (2,1)
Project Performance Measurement Plan (2,1)
Location Model View (2,2)
Organization Model View (2,2)
Other Organizational Reports (2,2)
Staffing Plans (2,2)
Monitoring and Tracking (2,3)
Other (Special Purpose) Development Plans (2,3)
Other Feasibility and Analysis Reports (2,3)
_Null[17] (Operational / Process) (3,1)
_Null (Operational / People) (3,2)
_Null (Operational / Technology) (3,3)

COMMUNICATIONS DEVELOPMENT

Logical Business Process Hierarchy, Definitions & Events (1,1)
Proposed Business Change Reports (1,1)
Value Chain Analysis (1,1)
Customer & User Needs / Process Matrix (1,1)
Stakeholder Model (1,2)
Stakeholder Communication and Enrollment Plan (1,2)
_Null (Strategic / Technology) (1,3)
Other Supporting Plans for Project Management (2,1)
Project Management Plan (2,1)
Organization Model View (2,2)
Organizational Change Plan (2,2)
Other Organizational Reports (2,2)
Staffing Plans (2,2)
Monitoring and Tracking (2,3)
Other (Special Purpose) Development Plans (2,3)
Release Plans (3,1)
Issue Management (3,1)
Document Management (3,1)
Organizational Change Unit Review Plan (3,2)
On-Duty List (3,2)
Quality Management Work Products (3,3)
Risk Management Work Products (3,3)

[17] A _Null component implies none exists for that dimension.

Enterprise Transformation

Data Model Views, Flows, et al. (1,1)
Logical Business Process Hierarchy, Definitions & Events (1,1)
Conceptual Flow Diagrams (1,1)
Proposed Business Change Reports (1,1)
Value Chain Analysis (1,1)
Business Process Principles, Constraints & Assumptions (1,1)
Customer & User Needs / Process Matrix (1,1)
Process / Function Map, Criticality Map & Flow Diagram (1,1)
Conceptual Business Event & Results Definitions (1,1)
BP Value and Performance Models (1,1)
Organizational Transition Plan (1,2)
Stakeholder Model (1,2)
Stakeholder Communication and Enrollment Plan (1,2)
Organizational Change Measurement Plan (1,2)
Application Portfolio Assessment (1,3)
Application Architecture (1,3)
Legacy Transformation Strategy (1,3)
Procurement Work Products (1,3)
Technology Model View (1,3)
IT Strategic Plan (1,3)
Program Dependencies (2,1)
Program Management Plan (2,1)
Business Transformation Plan (2,1)
Business Transformation Model (2,1)
Organization Model View (2,2)
Transition Model (2,2)
Staff Management Work Products (2,2)
Organizational Change Plan (2,2)
Other Organizational Reports (2,2)
Program Management Organization (2,2)
Staffing Plans (2,2)
Development Products (2,3)
Monitoring and Tracking (2,3)
Other (Special Purpose) Development Plans (2,3)
Other Feasibility and Analysis Reports (2,3)
Application Transformation Model (2,3)
Technology Transformation Model (2,3)
System Engineering Model View (2,3)
Issue Management (3,1)
Enterprise Transformation Plans (3,1)
Release Plans (3,1)
Deployment Site Plans (3,1)
Other Operational and Post-Transition Reports (3,1)
Disaster Recovery and Contingency Plans (3,1)
Document Management (3,1)
Configuration Management (3,1)
Organizational Change Unit Review Plan (3,2)
On-Duty List (3,2)
Data Transformation Model (3,2)
Physical Application Transformation (3,3)
Operations System Support Plan (3,3)
Quality Management Work Products (3,3)
Risk Management Work Products (3,3)

COTS Package Upgrade

Data Model Views, Flows, et al. (1,1)
Logical Business Process Hierarchy, Definitions, and Events (1,1)
Customer & User Needs / Process Matrix (1,1)
Process / Function Map, Criticality Map
Transition Model (2,2)
Review and Inspection Materials (2,2)
Staff Management Work Products (2,2)
Monitoring and Tracking (2,3)
Other Feasibility and Analysis Reports (2,3)

& Flow Diagram (1,1)
Acceptance Plan for Program Management (1,2)
Application Architecture (1,3)
Technology Model View (1,3)
Project Management Plan (2,1)
Other Supporting Plans for Project Management (2,1)
Template Site Deployment Plan (2,1)
Project Completion and Acceptance Plan (2,1)
Test Plans and Materials (2,1)
System Requirements Model (2,3)
Application Model View (2,3)
Configuration Management (3,1)
Release Plans (3,1)
Deployment Site Plans (3,1)
Other Operational and Post-Transition Reports (3,1)
Document Management (3,1)
Issue Management (3,1)
Data Transformation Model (3,2)
Operations System Support Plan (3,3)
Risk Management Work Products (3,3)

■ ■ ■

As you develop frameworks for Asset Types, you'll recognize matching *components*. That is to be expected. Many components are similar because the working parts of many *Asset Types* are the same. Therefore, it is important to develop standards for both Asset Types and Components increasing their reuse value and minimizing their creation costs.

Not only that, with standards you can reduce training costs, knowledge transfer costs, employee turnover costs, while you increase productivity and shorten delivery times. All of which reduce project costs and reduce risks.

Bonus I | Capability Mapping

Throughout our work as participants in projects, as project managers, and as portfolio managers, we realized that many failure points are tied directly to people. Specifically, people who lacked the skills, or who had the skills but for other issues did not deliver on their responsibilities. However, as we saw it, it wasn't always one person, but a poorly performing team, due to a lack of cohesion. Strong cohesion makes up for inevitable weaknesses among team members.

With our 9dimensions framework, it wasn't sufficient to tie roles and responsibilities to components. We needed to develop a better method for evaluating and building *teams*.

THE IMPETUS

We came across several papers on the science of *protein folding* and its *gamification*. The application of game playing to protein folding was of interest, but of more interest was that through a gaming process of trial and error, with little knowledge, a better protein fold could be found, where folded proteins are held together by various molecular *interactions*. Interactions being key.

Without getting deep into either topic, we realized when companies put together teams, they rarely consider team cohesion, or potential *interactions* between the team members as a means by which they assemble teams. And if they do, it is at a holistic level not taking into account *roles*, but titles only.

Our next step took us deeper into the software side of protein folding, not to study the science or the gamification, but to better understand molecular modelling (Figure 27), Chemical Markup Language (CML), and other software that allow for viewing, validation, and manipulating chemical structures.

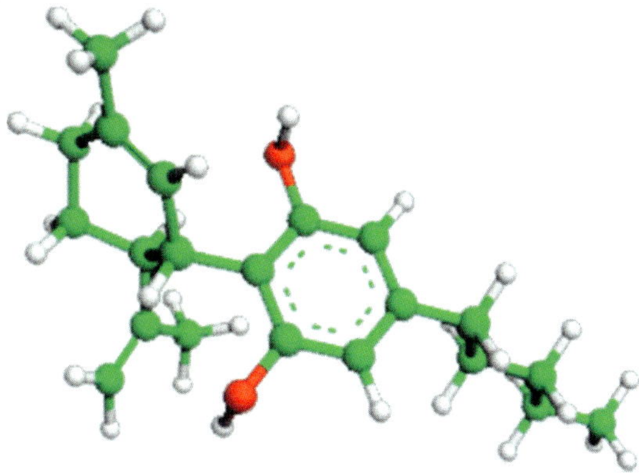

Figure 27 - Chemical Markup Language (CML)

We decided that teams do not differ from a complex chemical structure, and to maintain cohesion, there had to be a better model for bonding, and building cohesion. There had to exist a way to bond teammates with disparate personalities in such a way to maintain cohesion during easy and hard times, during moments of agreement and disagreement, and over the long haul.

A HUMAN CAPITAL CHEMISTRY SET

PERSONALITY TRAITS

We began our journey studying an existing catalog[18] and grouping of personality traits, to determine cohesion by traits. The 600+ traits made it impossible to efficiently *markup* teams.

We next studied a collection of personality and social styles such as

---

[18] e.g., Positive: Accessible, Adaptable, Clever, + 230 more; Neutral: Amusing, Artful, Enigmatic, + 290 more; Negative: Abrasive, Abrupt, Angry, + 290 more

Myers-Briggs, DISC, and others; settling on a simple Merrill-Reid framework with two spectrums: degree of Extroversion-Introversion *and* preference for People or Tasks, which puts people into one of four groups for their primary style: *Analytical*, *Driver*, *Amiable*, and *Expressive*.

- **Driver** Personality Types
    - Are competitive and want to win
    - Always look for control and to take over control
    - Are quick in their actions and reactions
    - Are good at planning and being decisive
    - Are result-oriented and task-oriented
    - Don't like inefficiency and weak decisiveness
- **Analytic** Personality Types
    - Focus more on tasks than on people
    - Like to be right and take the time to show this
    - Are reflective, cautious, and precise
    - Are good at evaluating and solving problems
    - Are good at working alone, avoid group activities
    - Are careful when making decisions
    - Are critical and have low responsiveness
- **Expressive** Personality Styles
    - Intuitive, Creative, Enthusiastic
    - Spontaneous, Funny, and easily interact with others
    - Are afraid of being rejected
    - Love confirmation and praise
    - Don't like routine and complex matters
    - Tend to generalize and exaggerate
    - Use a sarcastic tone when they're stressed

- **Amiable** Personality Styles
    - Listen attentively and excel at teamwork
    - Want to be respected and to be popular
    - Want to be seen as nice
    - Look for safety, stability and an organized workplace
    - Take their time to make decisions
    - Prefer following orders to taking the lead
    - Are afraid of change and uncertainty

Keep in mind that these are basic traits and we all have some of each in us. On the whole, we belong in one primary style but have a strong affinity for one of the other styles as our secondary and underlying trait (Figure 28).

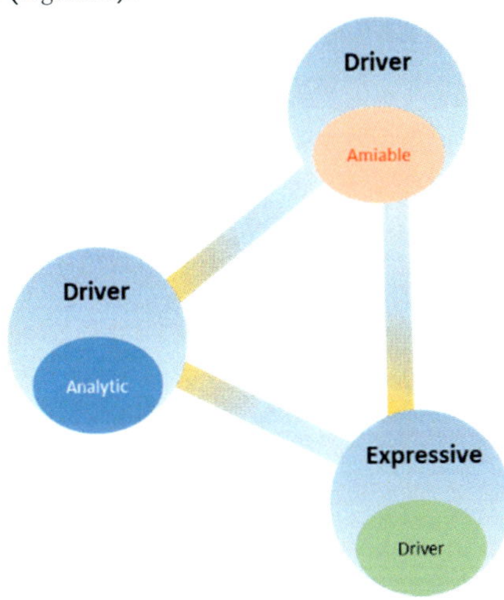

Figure 28 - Team Cohesion

There is a pathway (Figure 29) we follow between the different styles as we face a *fight-or-flight* mode. It's been our experience that the path traveled by people follows the bi-directional red line in personality types.

For example, when a driver faces strong opposition, they move to analytic (i.e., trying to rationalize), then to expressive (i.e., yelling and screaming), and finally to amiable (i.e., they shut up and comply.)

On the other hand, if we put an Amiable into a corner, they move towards expressive (i.e., speaking up), then to analytic (i.e., rationalizing their demands), and finally to driver (i.e., ordering people around and taking charge.)

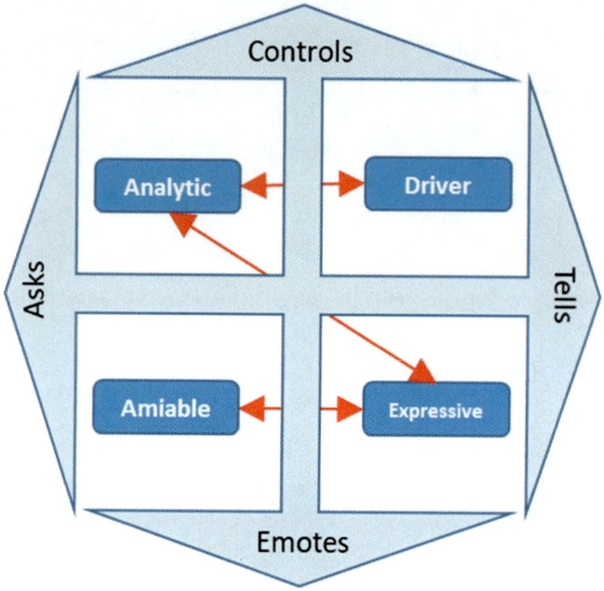

Figure 29 - Personality Types

The one thing we learned quickly is that personality traits within a project correlate strongly to a *role*, and not title. A person will exhibit different styles depending on their role. For example, a person may be comfortable being a *driver* in the role of a "project manager" but feel better as an *analytic* in the role of an "analyst" and perhaps even an *amiable* as a "programmer" in a language in which they are not well versed.

POLITICAL APTITUDE

Personality traits are the first part of the cohesion function. The other area to consider is political aptitude, that a person can influence others through existing relationships and history in an area, or raw aptitude. This is not role-specific but more business entity or organizational and typically applies to consultative teams - internal or external. The categories are:

1. No Influence
2. Minor Influence
3. Major Influence
4. Inner Circle

THE MAPPING

Capability mapping for each employee now includes determining the traits they possess for each of the roles they might hold, and their overall general political aptitude. Traits can be evaluated and adjusted over time, but on day one it could be part of a skills matrix questionnaire. When on-boarding a new employee, it's prudent to take measure of their skills with a questionnaire (Figure 30) or a test.

Be careful, with your choices. Rarely do people want to admit they are "amiable" or "expressive." The choice of words should fit the culture in which the mapping occurs.

Role	Exp. (yrs.)	Driver	Analytic	Expressive	Amiable
Project Manager	10	❍ 1st ❍ 2nd	❍ 1st ❍ 2nd	❍ 1st ❍ 2nd	❍ 1st ❍ 2nd
Product Manager	10	❍ 1st ❍ 2nd	❍ 1st ❍ 2nd	❍ 1st ❍ 2nd	❍ 1st ❍ 2nd
C# Developer	10	❍ 1st ❍ 2nd	❍ 1st ❍ 2nd	❍ 1st ❍ 2nd	❍ 1st ❍ 2nd
Python Developer	4	❍ 1st ❍ 2nd	❍ 1st ❍ 2nd	❍ 1st ❍ 2nd	❍ 1st ❍ 2nd

Figure 30 - Roles Assessments

THE TEAM

With the mapping in place you can now develop teams that are more balanced. That is to say, depending on the roles you need to build and deliver the *components* in your *Asset Type*, pick people that can best support a cohesive team (Figure 31).

This process is complex, and an art form developed over years of practice. We won't discuss it here but will say that having all of one trait will be an utter failure. Equal parts of all will also fail, as would having drivers at the bottom and an amiable at the top (sometimes!)

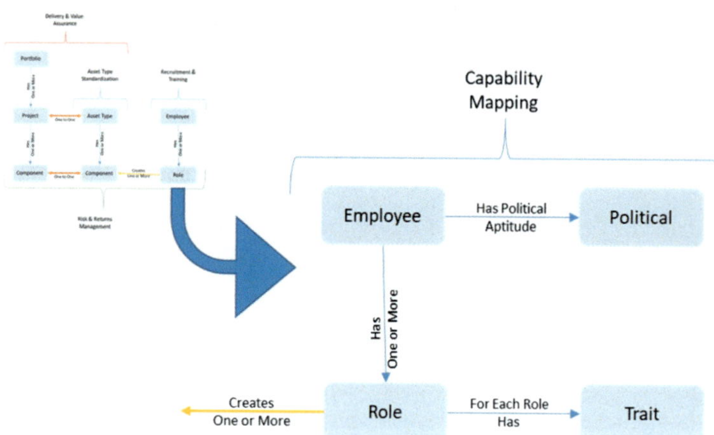

Figure 31 - ERM with Capability Mapping

Bonus II | Surveys

Over the years, we conducted hundreds of surveys on the topics of Portfolio and Project Management, Program Management setup and evaluation, and for specific client projects. The domain, depth, and breadth of surveys varied greatly, but they all had, at a minimum, the following set of questions as mandatory, for which we collected over 57,800 sets of answers.

SURVEY QUESTIONS

Given the ***9dimensions*** framework and ***Existence*** definition, we asked survey participants to answer:

- **Questions 1-9** | for each of the nine dimensions, tell us if the deliverables (components) existed or not, on a scale of one (1) [did not exist at all] to five (5) [fully existed.] The response mechanism was a slider allowing for incremental steps of 1/10 from one to five, allowing for granularity.
- **Question 10** | was the project successful? One (1) [a complete failure] and five (5) [a complete success.] The response mechanism for this question was bubble choices with five options and no granularity.

The answers to Q1-Q10 were subjective and not verified by us. We wanted to get a *feel* for what people *thought*. Ultimately, we wanted to see if there was any inherent intelligence built into the thought process. Moreover, do or can people associate *existence* with *success* or *failure*.

We present the answers for each dimension as a distribution across our scale, 1 to 5. However, we do not use a *normal* distribution model with evenly sized *bins*. Instead, we use the *Bayesian Blocks* binning strategy. This strategy allows for different size bins across the scale (1-5) in such a manner as to present clusters more prominently. Next, we present the correlations between the 10 answers. Finally, we dig deep into the data to check for *signs of intelligence*.

DELIVERABLES DISTRIBUTION

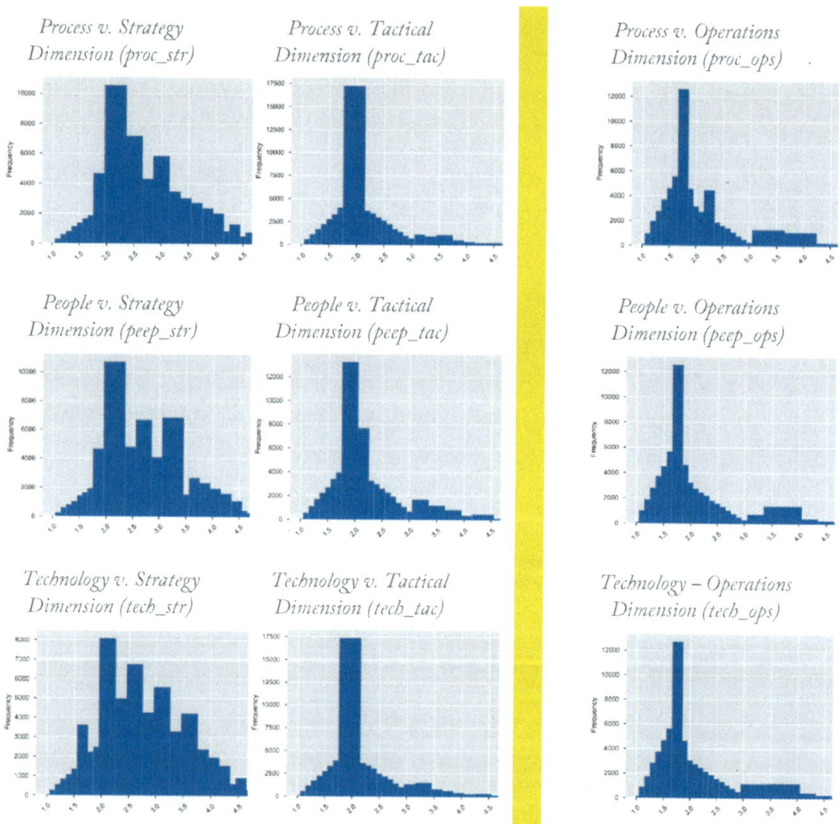

The vertical yellow line shows the Event Horizon. Overall, the charts skew to the left, with a broader spread in strategic deliverables, and thinning as the projects evolve. And, once the project moves past the event horizon the deliverables get sparser. This is in line with actual results.

PROJECT RESULTS (FAILURE V. SUCCESS)

Most projects fall in the middle (mean=2.72) with a standard deviation of 0.52, and skew towards failure (skew = -0.44), as per our actual findings. As expected, very few thought a project a complete success or failure. However, nearly a third (29.6%) thought it closer to a failure, than the 2.1% that thought it closer to a success (Figure 32).

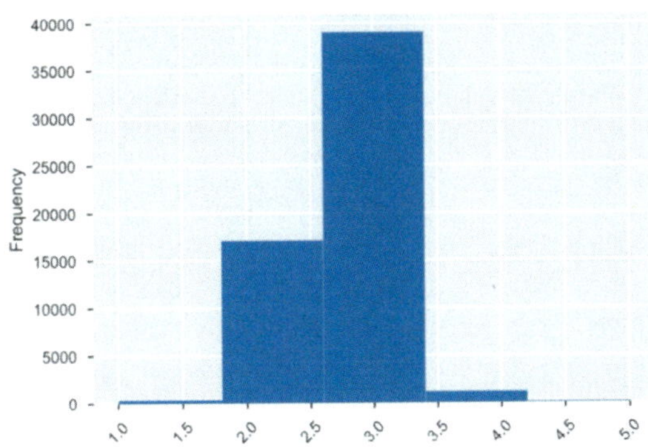

Figure 32 - Survey Results

Minimum	1	Standard Deviation	0.52
5th percentile	2	COEF of Variation	0.19
Q1	2	Kurtosis	0.36
Median	3	Mean	2.72
Q3	3	MAD	0.45
95th percentile	3	Skewness	-0.44
Maximum	5	Variance	0.29
Range	4		
Interquartile range	1		

Value	Count	Freq.
3	39,045	67.6%
2	17,082	29.6%
4	1,197	2.1%
1	374	0.6%
5	102	0.2%

CORRELATIONS

A *Pearson Correlation* (Figure 33) are values between -1 and 1 that show the extent to which two variables are linearly related.

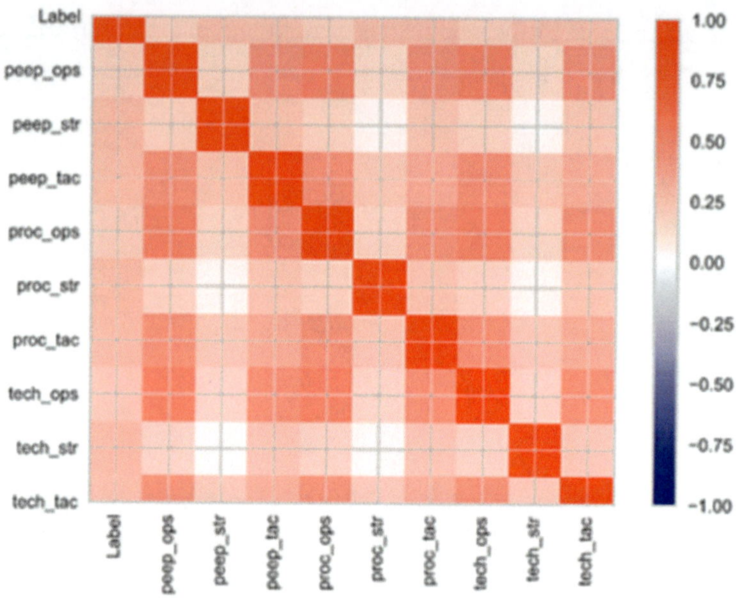

Figure 33 - Pearson Correlation

Phi(k) Correlations (Figure 34), in contrast, are a new correlation coefficient based on refinements to Pearson's model, and present an advantage over existing coefficients: *First*, it works consistently between categorical, ordinal, and interval variables. *Second*, it captures non-linear dependency. *Third*, it reverts to the Pearson correlation coefficient in case of a bi-variate normal input distribution. In both models, the correlations are above zero, as expected, implying a positive relationship between existence and success, and existence in general.

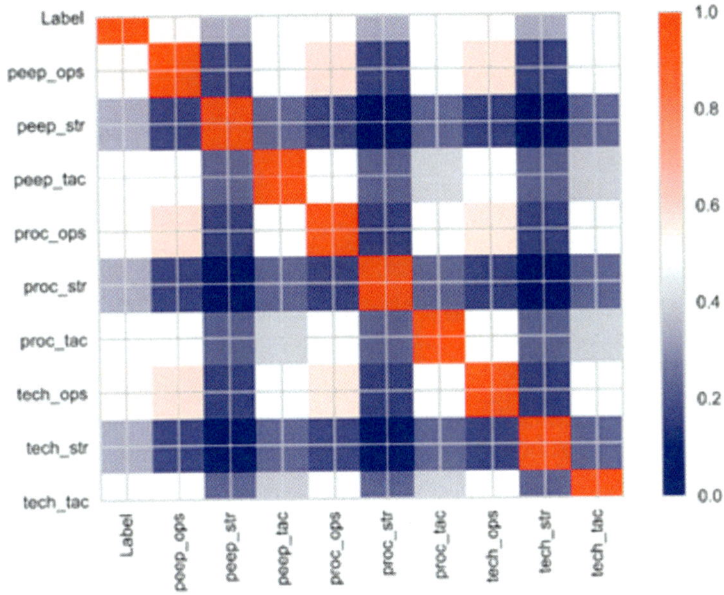

Figure 34 - Phi(k) Correlation

DERIVED INTELLIGENCE

Given our collected survey results, we took it upon ourselves to dig deeper into the data, applying Machine Learning models to gauge if there are useful and applicable models hidden deep in the data.

Machine Learning (ML) is becoming ubiquitous in our lives and is a hot topic of late. This book will not explore the science, nor will it be a tutorial on the subject. ML is math (i.e., calculus, linear algebra, and statistics) brilliantly coded into algorithms and packaged into libraries[19] which are used to develop predictive *models*.

The input into these *models* is data, split in two parts: *Features* (i.e., model input) and *Labels* (i.e., model results, output, or predictions).

19 e.g., Numpy, Pandas, Scikit-Learn, PyTorch, Keras, TensorFlow, etc.

For example,

- Features can be facial geometry and labels can be names.
- Features can be pixels in an image and labels can be an animal or clothing type.
- Features can be economic data and labels can be degrees of recession.
- Features can be details about homes and labels can be home prices.

In our case, *features* are the *existence values* (i.e., components did or did not exist) for each of the dimensions and *labels* are the *project outcome* (i.e., failure or success.)

SHALLOW LEARNING

We categorize most traditional and well tested models that have been around for quite some time as *Shallow Learning*, contrasting them with Deep Learning about which we'll speak later. We have spent a great deal of time studying, testing, and deploying many of the models, tools, and techniques. Commercially, there are new or improved libraries being packaged and productized monthly. For the first portion of our ML section we used PyCaret[20], an open source modeling toolkit based on Scikit-Learn[21] and Python.

Let's start with basic terms and definitions.

- **True Positive** (TP) = an outcome where the model *correctly* predicts the *positive class*.
- **True Negative** (TN) = an outcome where the model *correctly* predicts the *negative class*.
- **False Positive** (FP, Type 1 Error) = an outcome where the model *incorrectly* predicts the *positive class*.
- **False Negative** (FN, Type 2 Error) = an outcome where the model *incorrectly* predicts the *negative class*.

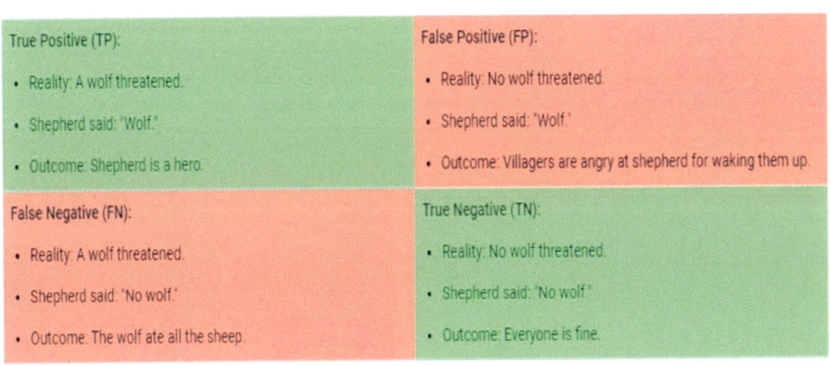

Figure 35 - Confusions Matrix Wolf Example

---

20 Visit https://github.com/pycaret/pycaret to learn more.
21 Visit https://scikit-learn.org/ to learn more.

Define "Wolf" (Figure 35) as a *positive class* and "No Wolf" as a *negative class*. Remember, Actual Values are *true or false*, and Predicted Values are *positive or negative*. Therefore,

- **Precision** [TP / (TP + FP)] is number of times you said wolf over all instances of a wolf being there or not.
- **Recall** [TP / (TP + FN)] is number of times you said wolf over all instances of a wolf actually being there.
- **Accuracy** [(TP+TN)/(TP+TN+FP+FN)] is the number of correct predictions out of all predictions.

Combine it all into the F1-Score as such (the higher the better), or keep it as the Confusion Matrix (Figure 36):

Predicted Values \ Actual Values	Positive (1)	Negative (0)
Positive (1)	TP	FP
Negative (0)	FN	TN

$$F1 = 2 \times \frac{Recall \times Precision}{Recall + Precision}$$

Figure 36 - Confusion Matrix

Finally, the Kappa[22] score (the higher the better), is a metric that compares an Observed Accuracy with an Expected Accuracy (random chance).

[22] Visit https://en.wikipedia.org/wiki/Cohen%27s_kappa to learn more.

We ran fifteen models, with 10-fold cross validation, on 70% of the data, keeping 30% for validation, and sorted by the F1-Score.

Model	Accuracy	Recall	Precision	F1	Kappa
CatBoost Classifier	0.916	0.398	0.901	0.907	0.811
Light Gradient Boosting Machine	0.906	0.389	0.892	0.897	0.788
Extra Trees Classifier	0.901	0.369	0.883	0.889	0.772
K Neighbors Classifier	0.891	0.401	0.883	0.886	0.755
Gradient Boosting Classifier	0.896	0.372	0.879	0.885	0.759
Extreme Gradient Boosting	0.897	0.363	0.878	0.883	0.759
Random Forest Classifier	0.883	0.379	0.871	0.876	0.734
Naive Bayes	0.856	0.472	0.899	0.865	0.685
Ada Boost Classifier	0.854	0.348	0.836	0.843	0.664
Decision Tree Classifier	0.807	0.416	0.874	0.837	0.602
Quadratic Discriminant Analysis	0.806	0.427	0.833	0.811	0.575
SVM - Linear Kernel	0.831	0.319	0.822	0.81	0.586
Logistic Regression	0.786	0.295	0.759	0.764	0.474
Linear Discriminant Analysis	0.771	0.313	0.758	0.756	0.452
Ridge Classifier	0.773	0.284	0.748	0.746	0.429

It is possible to extract a model from the data supporting a connection between *existence* and project results. However, before popping the champagne, know that imbalanced data sets, which this is, are not the best starting point for an outstanding model. The best data sets have equal parts, amounts of data, for each label.

Given that project results will always be a bell-shaped curve you have several options:

- Use what you have, as is, knowing the model will be weaker for fast results.
- Convert the labels into even sized bins and run a classification model.
- Convert the labels into percentages and run a regression model.

From our fifteen models we chose the best, the CatBoost[23] Classifier, and further tuned it looking for improvements.

	Accuracy	Recall	Precision	F1	Kappa
0	0.93	0.41	0.92	0.92	0.84
1	0.91	0.41	0.90	0.91	0.81
2	0.91	0.40	0.90	0.90	0.80
3	0.92	0.40	0.90	0.91	0.81
4	0.92	0.40	0.90	0.91	0.81
5	0.92	0.40	0.91	0.91	0.82
6	0.92	0.40	0.91	0.91	0.82
7	0.92	0.40	0.90	0.91	0.81
8	0.91	0.40	0.90	0.90	0.80
9	0.91	0.42	0.90	0.91	0.81
Mean	0.92	0.40	0.90	0.91	0.81
SD	0.0048	0.0066	0.0046	0.0045	0.0105

[23] CatBoost is a high-performance open source library for gradient boosting on decision trees. Visit https://catboost.ai to learn more.

The final Confusion Matrix (Figure 37):

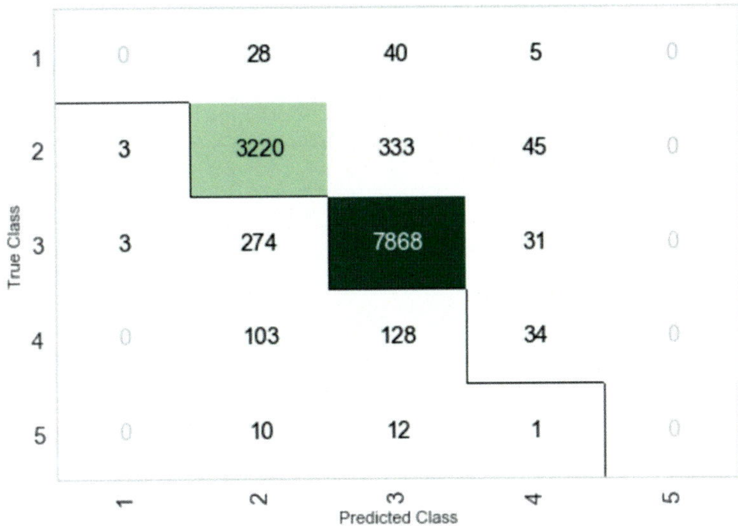

Figure 37 - CatBoost Confusion Matrix

The final Classification Report (Figure 38):

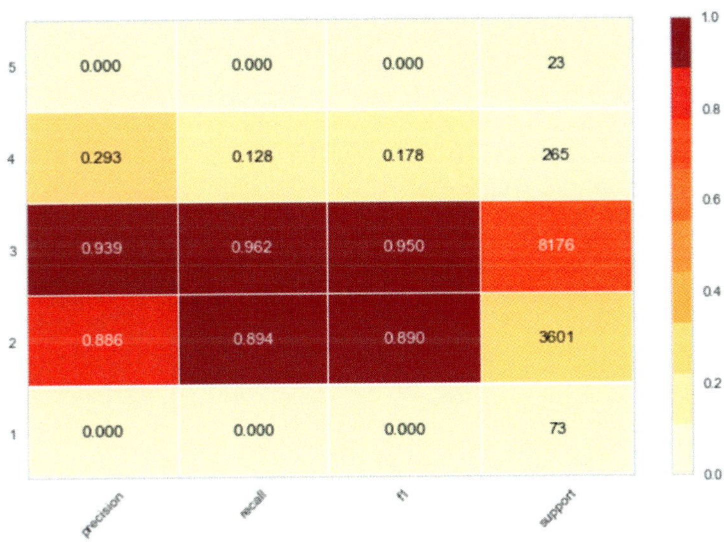

Figure 38 - CatBoost Classification Report

The final Prediction Error (Figure 39):

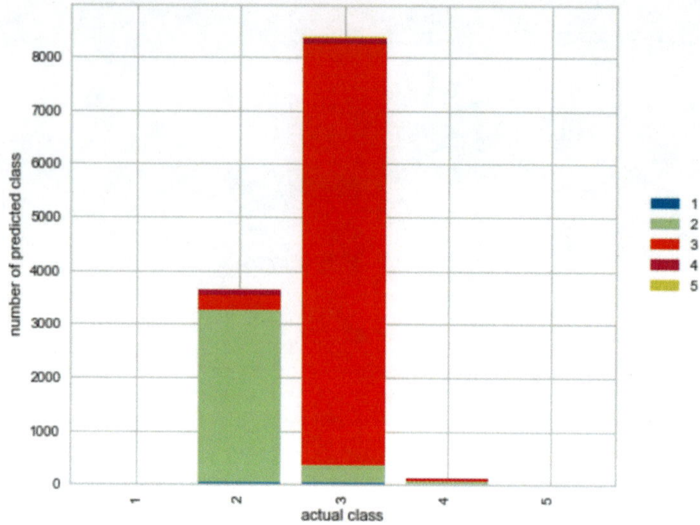

Figure 39 - CatBoost Prediction Error

DEEP LEARNING

Again, before we draw any conclusions, let us go deeper.

Deep Learning is a sub-field of machine learning in Artificial Intelligence (AI) that deals with algorithms inspired from the biological structure and functioning of a brain to aid machines with intelligence. It can further be defined as the process of bringing intelligence into a system or machine without *explicit* programming.

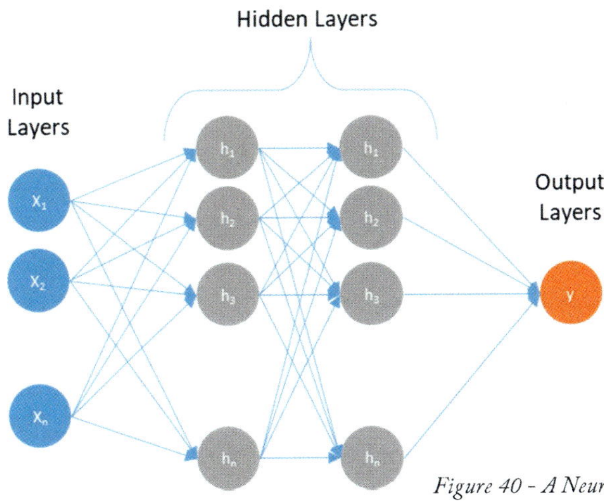

Figure 40 - A Neural Network

The word deep does not come from intellectual depth but more from the fact that we use many layers, hence deep (Figure 40), of data to reshape and process relationships to derive and extract models.

This all culminates in a popular area, that of Neural Networks[24] and the many variations thereof.

For this portion we used another tool based on open source called Deep Cognition[25], which wraps around Keras, TensorFlow, and other libraries to do its job.

---

24 Visit https://en.wikipedia.org/wiki/Artificial_neural_network to learn more.

25 Visit https://deepcognition.ai/ to learn more.

We'll go overboard on this and create many hidden layers (Figure 41), although two would suffice, to further improve the top scores we had with the *Shallow Learning* models earlier in this section.

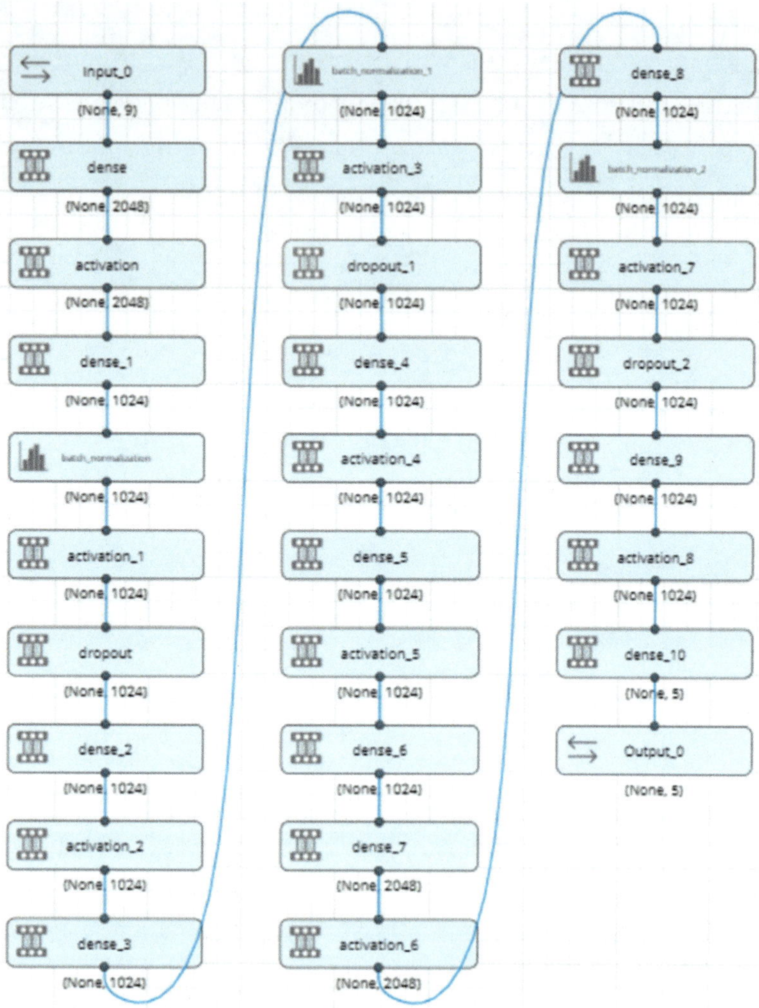

Figure 41 - Our Neural Network (NN) Model

Each layer is a building block in deep learning. It is a container that receives weighted inputs, transforms it with a set of mostly non-linear functions, and then passes these values as output to the next layer. Through this process we derive relationships.

We used *Categorical Cross Entropy* as the loss function and *Adadelta* as the optimizer, running 10 epochs with a batch size of 32 and a 70% train (40460), 15% validate (8670), and 15% test (8670) split.

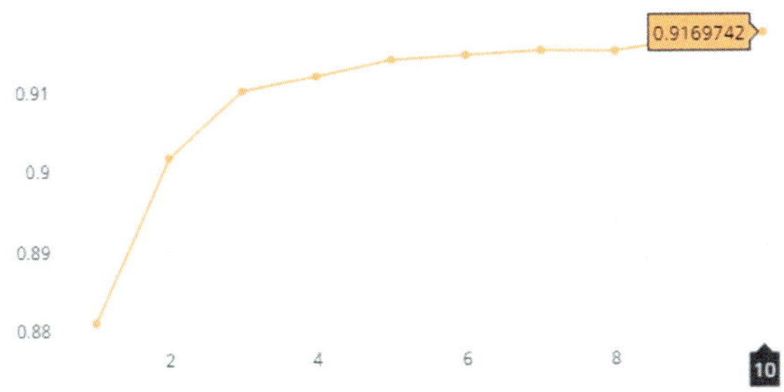

Figure 42 - NN Validation Accuracy

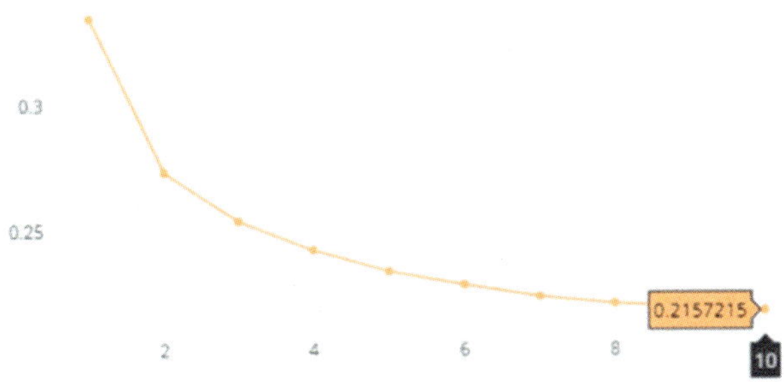

Figure 43 - NN Validation Loss

As mentioned before, imbalanced data sets do not make for the best models. So, we drew a line in the sand and converted our 5 project outcome labels (1-5) into two buckets, *pass* and *fail*. We then hand coded a simple and small Neural Network, using Keras on TensorFlow to see if there is an even better fitting model that can be derived.

```
import TensorFlow as tf
from TensorFlow import keras
from keras import Sequential
from keras.layers import Dense
from keras.callbacks import EarlyStopping, TensorBoard
#Early Stop and Tensorboard callbacks
es = EarlyStopping(monitor='val_loss', mode='min', verbose=1,
patience=10)
tensb = TensorBoard(log_dir = 'SimLogs')
#build model
model = Sequential()
model.add(Dense(32, activation='relu', input_dim=9))
model.add(Dense(1, activation='sigmoid'))
model.compile(loss='binary_crossentropy', optimizer = 'adam',
metrics = ['accuracy'])
model.fit(X.values, y.values, batch_size = 32, epochs = 20,
validation_split = 0.2, callbacks = [es, tensb])
model.summary()
```

Results of our Neural Network.

Epoch 1/20 - 9s 198us/step - loss: 0.4476 - accuracy: 0.8246 - val_loss: 0.3183 - val_accuracy: 0.8539

Epoch 2/20- 8s 183us/step - loss: 0.2339 - accuracy: 0.9188 - val_loss: 0.1747 - val_accuracy: 0.9701

....

Epoch 19/20- 9s 187us/step - loss: 0.0377 - accuracy: 0.9894 - val_loss: 0.0513 - val_accuracy: 0.9749

Epoch 20/20- 9s 185us/step - loss: 0.0367 - accuracy: 0.9892 -

val_loss: 0.0402 - val_accuracy: 0.9815

Model: "sequential_1"

Total params: 353, **Trainable params**: 353, **Non-trainable params**: 0

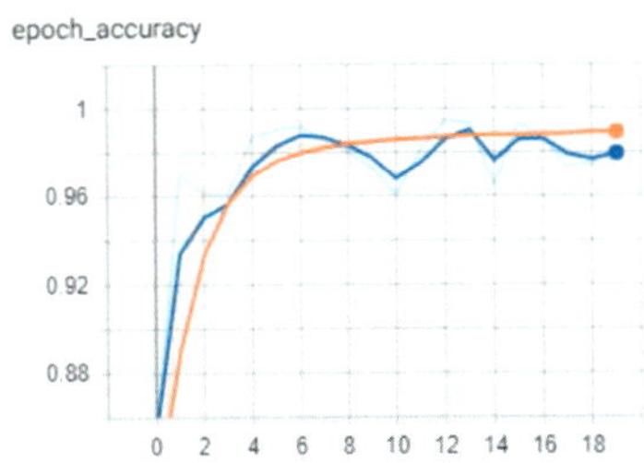

Figure 44 - Final NN Accuracy

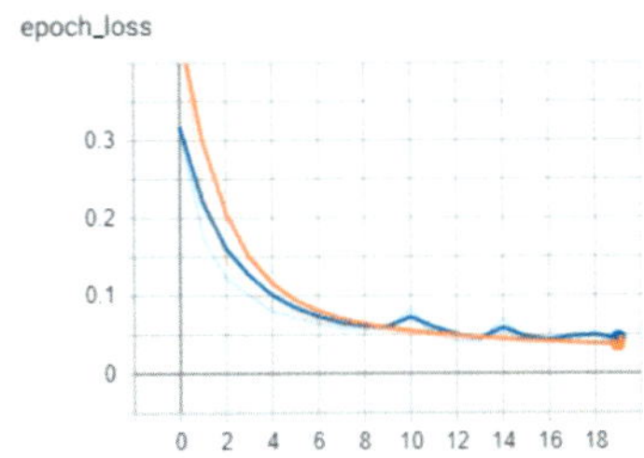

Figure 45 - Final NN Loss

Indeed, there was an improvement. We reached an accuracy level of 98.92%.

CONCLUSIONS

As mentioned at the start of this section, survey participants answered our questions without us verifying any part of it. We intended to collect what these folks *thought* based on facts known to them or based on their judgements alone. We collected baseline data for moving forward on other business relationships, amassing a trove of data before, during, and after the process of portfolio and program management.

The survey participants felt an association between success and the existence of supporting components and deliverables. They also confirmed the best work occurred in the beginning and waned as they moved towards, and beyond, the Event Horizon. They also confirmed that most projects lean towards failure by a large multiple.

Machine and Deep Learning are the Scientific Application of an Art Form

Examining this set of data does not require sophisticated business analytics or ML, due to the obvious and linear nature of the model. You are more likely to succeed as you prepare for and then create project deliverables (components). There is a strong correlation and causation between planning/preparing and success. The data naturally clusters into those recognizable areas. Are there better scenarios?

ML IN PROJECT ANALYSIS

The previous data structure is not best for ML. However, if you converted your dataset into a richer feature set, you will be on your way to a successful ML experience. Instead of using the 9dimensions framework, use all the components in practice at your company. You will go from nine features to many hundreds of features with binary values 1 (i.e., exists) and 0 (i.e., does not exist,) and your label will be pass or fail, with classification, or a percentage, with regression. Regression would be our choice.

In this new scenario you will have a powerful ML model for analyzing and predicting project failure rates. The feature set applies to *every* project but only the features in use will be checked off. Over time and through feature reduction, you will cut down on the total *components* as you learn which features (i.e., components) are most consequential to your success.

This is a growing practice area. However, it requires developing standard *Asset Types* with standard *Components*, used across the enterprise, with the following in mind:

- For every label (i.e., result, *y*), you must have ample and balanced data, to learn or categorize.
- It is not possible to use the actual results as they typically reside on a normal curve where extreme failures and successes *are not* the norm and what happens between the extremes *is* the norm, hence the bell curve.
- Labels must be a percentage or binary.

- Features[26] (X) should extend beyond the nine dimensions category allowing for models that are more complex, beyond linear models that fall on one side or the other.
- To achieve this, features can and should include at minimum all deliverables and components of a successful project, any project, (e.g., objectives analysis, project plans, cost benefit analysis, etc.), and have added features for specialized projects and only if there is ample data.
- It is possible to create hundreds of features, with *Existence* (1) / *Non-Existence* (0) as their values, working from a Sparse to a Dense Matrix.

HIRING PEOPLE FOR ML

There will come a time when you will look for and hire people for this art/science. Don't make the mistake of hiring based on tools knowledge. You will pay dearly.

This is required of the people whom you hire, in order of importance:

1. Hire people who have domain knowledge *or* the ability to quickly extract, collate, and validate domain knowledge; **and**
2. Hire people with a strong math background, specifically calculus, linear algebra, and statistics; **and**
3. Hire people who have *sufficient* and *variegated* programing skills, and who can quickly pick, choose, adapt, modify, and apply the ever growing and changing list of tools, libraries, and layers of abstraction.

Don't simply hire someone who knows Python, Scikit, Tensorflow, Caffe, PyTorch, Keras, or whatever the current hot tool is. This is akin to hiring a surgeon based mostly on their ability to cut and stitch with a specific branded scalpel and suturing kit.

---

26 Features are typically denoted by capital "X" signifying a matrix (i.e. many input values and weights), whereas the labels or results are denoted by lower case "y" signifying one value, the answer (e.g., cat or dog, yes or no, 23%, $48, etc.)

New tools and methods are born constantly. It can seem overwhelming or paralyzing. Start small and develop an in-house group dedicated to doing this, and only this.

Let it grow and evolve organically

About Us

M. MAX BOROUMAND ...

Max is a seasoned and experienced technologist, a futurist, and special advisor. His career spans over two decades, with clients in the Fortune 500, Governments, and non-profits, and many technology start-ups. His work and life have taken him all over the world, from the Middle East and North Africa, to Europe and the Americas, and to Asia. Over the last two decades, he has been the CEO of a holding company, whose portfolio includes several software companies, and a publishing and media company.

CHARLENE BOROUMAND ...

Charlene is an experienced management and technology consultant. Having graduated from MIT and Haas School of Business, she has spent equal parts in consulting, software start-ups, and the Fortune 500 in a variety of leadership positions. She is a persistently results-driven and outcome-oriented professional with extensive experience in process management, strategy & planning, organizational design, and transformational change. She believes nothing is impossible with proper effort and thought. She therefore thrives on helping companies innovate, differentiate, and successfully align investments to strategies and objectives.

OUR COMPANIES

In addition to our other responsibilities we are both principals in a Consultancy and Holding Company, Bit Economics, LLC, which has in its portfolio:

- 9dimensions, a software and consultancy company
- Daitum, an AI and ML consultancy
- Boroumand Mediart, a publishing company

BitEconomics.com

Delivery and Value Assurance™

Boroumand.com

Figures

Index

A

B

F

G

H

I

K

L

M

N

O

P

U

V

W

Made in the USA
Middletown, DE
23 September 2020

20404099R00071